BETS, DRUGS,
AND ROCK & ROLL

BETS, DRUGS, AND ROCK & ROLL

THE RISE AND FALL OF THE WORLD'S FIRST OFFSHORE SPORTS GAMBLING EMPIRE

STEVE BUDIN

with Bob Schaller

SKYHORSE PUBLISHING

www.skyhorsepublishing.com

Library of Congress Cataloging-in-Publication Data
Budin, Steve.
Bets, drugs, and rock & roll : the rise and fall of the world's first offshore sports gambling empire / Steve Budin with Bob Schaller.
p. cm.
Includes index.
ISBN 978-1-60239-099-7 (hardcover : alk. paper)
1. Sports betting. 2. Book-making (Betting) 3. Gambling. I. Schaller, Bob. II. Title. III. Title: Bets, drugs, and rock and roll.
GV717.B83 2007
796--dc22
2007024997

Printed in the United States of America

10 9 8 7 6 5 4 3 2 1

All events in *Bets, Drugs, and Rock & Roll* are true, and all characters are real. However, certain names have been changed to protect the identities of bettors and underworld figures.

ONE PERSON HAS dedicated and sacrificed everything she has for me. That person made me who I am in this book, who I am today, and who I am destined yet to be. That person is my mother, Rita Budin, "the crazy redhead from Williamsburg, Brooklyn."

She is brutally honest, tough as nails, and has the most incredible and infectious sense of humor. When she laughs, even the neighbors know! But most important, if anyone ever tried to harm me in any way, she'd wring their neck with her own bare hands. Knowing that you have someone in your corner who loves you like that is the essential ingredient to being a personal success in life.

So while my father is my mentor, my idol, my hero, and my best buddy, my mother is the *reason* I am, the *reason* I was, and the *reason* I will always be who I am. Thank you, Mama, I love you so much, and I hope, above all else, that you are proud of me. I dedicate this book, everything that came before it, and everything that comes after it, to you.

Contents

BETS, DRUGS,
AND ROCK & ROLL

Foreword

STEVE BUDIN IS a visionary.

What Steve Jobs was to the computer world, Steve Budin was—and continues to be—to the sports gambling industry. He has transformed what was once considered a dirty little secret into a mainstream phenomenon.

I'm not pitching you here. I'm stating the facts, and believe me, as a guy who has seen and participated in every aspect of the sports gambling business and had a movie, *Two for the Money,* made about his life, I'm going to give you the real deal and the bottom line on Mr. Budin—or "Stevo," as the privileged many he considers friends get to call him.

Sports gambling has been around since the early part of the twentieth century. But it was always a backroom industry. If you wanted to bet on the ponies, you went to the track. If you wanted to buy a lottery ticket, you went to your local Seven-Eleven. But if you wanted to wager on sports, you had to deal with your local bookmaker, the-here-today-gone-tomorrow crony who was most likely backed by the mob.

Steve Budin personally changed the way gamblers wager by

creating the offshore sportsbook industry. He made it possible to sit in the convenience and privacy of your home and use your credit card to wager on sports via the phone or Internet.

No more local bookies.

No more hoping you'll get paid if you win.

No more hoping your bookie didn't get busted by the cops before he paid you.

Steve reshaped a shady business overnight and made it respectable by changing the way gamblers bet on games. By bringing it into the mainstream, he made it an acceptable way of life for millions of casual gamblers worldwide.

Right now online poker is the rage, but understand this: Without Steve Budin's creation of the offshore sportsbook industry, there would be no online poker.

I had heard about Steve and his exploits many, many times but didn't actually meet him until 2003. Talk about getting blown away by first impressions. Gregarious, fun-loving—yes. But don't for a minute think I didn't realize I was having a sit-down with one of the sharpest business minds I'd ever encountered.

At the time, I was out of the gambling business, no longer selling my picks to anyone. I had grown tired of the shysters and high-pressure salesmen surrounding me for over a decade while selling my sports picks to customers in what is commonly known as a boiler-room operation.

The movie about my life and experiences in the sports handicapping business, *Two for the Money,* was about to go into production, and I missed picking games, making people money. But there was no way in hell I was going to return to the world dominated by shady salesmen pushing plays down gamblers' throats.

In 2003 Steve Budin changed my life.

Having created the offshore sportsbook industry, Steve had another goal in mind: revolutionizing the way handicappers, sold their picks to the public. And once again, the Internet was his medium of choice.

Steve flat-out told me that he wanted to become the "Wal-Mart of the sports handicapping industry," selling handicappers' selections and analysis online for a low price to the masses.

Was I skeptical at first? Of course I was. I mean, I had spent ten years in a business where salesmen would call potential customers morning, noon, and night, harassing them into buying one pick for $300 to $3,000. Yet here was Steve telling me the way to go was selling my selections online for $29.95.

My first thought was: *Are you kidding me?* Someone must have spiked the Diet Coke he kept gulping down!

Then he showed me his first two websites, WhoWill-Cover.com and SportsAdvisors.com, and told me how a handicapper with a movie about his life, a guy who had Matthew McConaughey playing him on the silver screen, could become the biggest handicapper in the world with his online sales platform and marketing/advertising strategies behind him.

On that day, BrandonLang.com was born, and true to his word, Steve made my dreams come true by giving me a platform to sell my selections to a worldwide audience at an affordable price with no salesmen, no middlemen, and no hype or scams. Steve gave me the courage to get back into the sports handicapping industry. He validated the industry with his simple, straight-to-the-point method of selling picks online.

I said at the outset that Steve is a visionary, and I mean that in the truest sense of the word. He literally took two tainted backroom businesses and brought them to mainstream acceptance, making them part of everyday life for millions of adults worldwide.

Without Steve, I'm not on ESPN when they want to discuss issues involving the sports gambling world.

Without Steve, I'm not doing thirty interviews on TV and radio weekly throughout the football season and during March Madness.

I have no idea what Steve's next mountain will be to climb, but whatever it is, I've got his back and I'm ready to roll large with him.

Some guys see the big picture. Steve Budin dreams it, and then turns it into reality.

—Brandon Lang
May 21, 2007

BETS, DRUGS,
AND ROCK & ROLL

1

From Beaches to Behind Bars

SO THIS IS where it all ends.

In a New York City jail cell.

Come to think of it, that's not all that far from where it all began, on the rough-and-tumble streets of Brooklyn, where our original bookmaking shop was located. The guys who worked the phones for us there would always keep one eye on the betting slips and the other on the door, knowing damn well that the law could show up at any moment and kick it down.

As I sat in that jail cell with my father—a bench on either side, a toilet in the middle—I knew it wasn't the end of the world, only the end of the wildest ride of my life. I started out as a Brooklyn-bred street bookie who was able—as a teen—to help grow his father's bookmaking business in Florida into one of the biggest bookmaking operations on the entire East Coast. I learned the business by handling the "pay-and-collects" for my father, all the while building up my own list of private clients. I never thought that I would end up becoming the biggest bookmaker in the world or forever change the way people bet on sports.

But all good things come to an end, and as my father and I sat there in the cell, we smiled at each other. It wasn't like we were up on murder charges. The charge was a count of simple bookmaking.

Unfortunately, that was the only thing that was simple.

I had built, from the ground up, the first and biggest offshore bookmaking business in the world, raking in millions of dollars every month, first in Panama and then in Costa Rica.

Bookmaking is, of course, illegal in the United States. People do it anyway. Some say it's bad for you, but so is smoking. Drinking, too. Both of those are legal, and the government takes in billions a year in "sin" taxes.

Of course, I wasn't in the United States when I ran my offshore operation, but a simple fact that every American should be aware of is that you can be prosecuted for crimes under U.S. law wherever you are in the world. My case was considered a "gray area" because most of my clients were in the United States, where telephone sports betting is illegal, even though I was located in another country where offering bets via telephone was completely legal.

I left a billion-dollar deal on my desk the day I came back home to surrender to the FBI. Yes, a one followed by nine zeros—a deal that would turn into what is now the multibillion-dollar empire known as www.sportsbook.com.

I started my business with literally nothing except the knowledge I had accrued in the gambling business. Hundreds of millions of dollars and four years after it all began, it was time to pay the piper—and why not? Everyone else had already gotten their piece of me.

. . .

BEFORE THE FEDS came knocking, we at my company, SDB Global in Costa Rica, were approaching what would be our last football season. I was so focused on the future expansion of my business that I never could have seen the split-finger fastball the government was about to throw at me, let alone prepare myself for it.

Sandy Berger, a Miami lawyer and former public defender, was my best friend from Miami at that time. I brought him into the business with me from the very beginning in Panama, and he remains a dear friend and respected colleague to this day. Ironically, as his job at SDB Global became less and less intensive day to day (because our systems were so solid), he started to use his time to do research on U.S. gambling laws and the political climate surrounding offshore betting, which had already become a highly controversial subject around D.C. with both lobbyists and lawmakers. By this time we weren't the only players in the game. There were, I believe, eighteen competitors who ran half-assed operations in places like Antigua and Saint Kitts and a few other start-ups that followed my lead in Costa Rica. We were certainly the big fish swimming in the little pond otherwise known as the offshore sports betting industry. One of our bigger problems was that these little fish were turning our pond into a cesspool with their deceptive and dishonest business practices: not paying people and messing with credit customers through undesirable U.S. intermediaries (betting agents) who would pay and collect on the offshore sportsbooks' behalf—in the United States—in cash, and in violation of every law on the books. We didn't want to be lumped in with those losers, and we weren't: we were considered the top echelon within the industry—an industry that was growing at such an astounding rate that it was becoming just too big to be ignored.

Each day Sandy would e-mail me the arguments going on in the U.S. Congress regarding offshore gambling or anything else related to telephone and Internet sports betting. What a pain in my ass he was: If any two-bit bookmaker got arrested anywhere in the United States, Sandy would document it and put it on my desk. I really didn't pay much attention to Sandy's paranoia and just chalked it up to his criminal law background, general cynicism, and constant overevaluation process that became his mantra toward the end. I certainly understood Sandy's anxiety as our lawyer, but as the shit started to hit the fan, he had his rubber gloves on so tight that they were cutting off the circulation to *my* brain.

On the recommendation of one of our U.S. lawyers, we hired private investigator Paul Pringles, a retired FBI agent who sold us on his ability to gauge what was going on within the FBI through his "contacts." His girlfriend was an active FBI agent, and he referred to her as "Cookie," which we knew wasn't her real name. Pringles would speak directly with her and then relay the information to us. When he contacted her to try to get a feel for whether offshore gambling was on their radar, she relayed the following:

> The only department that has ever prosecuted a gambling case is the Organized Crime Division. After speaking in great detail to the heads of those departments, who are my friends, and confirming that the Organized Crime Division of the FBI has no interest in offshore gambling (unless it is mob-related), I would say that you are currently operating in a "gray area" with little to no risk at this time.

Pringles explained to us that the FBI had its hands full with black-and-white "prosecutable" crimes that were occurring on American soil and simply couldn't waste time chasing after "gray areas" abroad. With those types of high-level assurances, I really wasn't worried about the U.S. government. I always felt that we would get enough notice to be able to get out in time, if it ever came to that.

A change was occurring in the bookmaking business, technologically driven change, and all of it was steered toward the Internet. Up to the point where it became "transactional" (in its infancy the Internet was nothing but a business card—a billboard for businesses, if you will) 100 percent of all bets in the world were taken via telephone. But when we added an online sign-up option, I noticed that up to one-quarter of our new clients came from those Internet sign-up forms. We were making millions a month off the phones, but I was spending a ton of money to operate this beast of an operation. I knew that we were reaching our capacity as a phone-driven business; I couldn't expand my telephone operation any more without sacrificing the quality of service and the level of control and security we had with the two hundred clerks we were operating with at that moment. To think that I once considered myself a real big shot, paying and collecting in the streets of Miami (as a teen and then a twenty-year-old) for a three-hundred-customer bookmaking operation that wrote the bets out of my friend Tony's Brooklyn basement apartment with seven phone clerks. Now I was servicing nine thousand active customers on two hundred phones and nearing technological capacity. You think my ego wasn't the size of the Chrysler Building? I could have jerked off to a mere reflection of myself in my computer screen. It was such a high. And as high as I was on myself, I was equally determined to keep it all going and to stay on top. I was never going to waste my time patting myself on the back at the cost of missing out on what was to come. The Internet was like a messiah for a company like mine, which was looking for a new technology to embrace—a technology that would make the cost of expansion and operation almost *zero* while driving the bottom line sky-high. With no significant overhead in clerks, computers, and space, all of the money would go directly into our net profit.

So I grabbed on to the Internet concept with both hands and squeezed it like a $50 Costa Rican hooker from the famous Hotel Del Ray in downtown San José. I mean, think about it for a second: We were taking minimum bets of $50 on the phones most of the time, and $100 minimums whenever it was twenty minutes or less before game time. That was when our phones were jammed with gamblers, and I just could not afford to have someone who was trying to bet thousands of dollars get a busy signal while some other guy was tying up our lines betting $50 a game.

If we could offer betting on the Internet, it wouldn't matter how many bettors there were at once, because nobody would ever get a busy signal! We could take $2 bets from thousands of people at the same time, so it wouldn't matter how big or little the bets were. I knew this would be great, because when we started posting our lines on our website for our customers to see, the traffic poured in. Nobody could understand why; I wondered the same thing. Why would someone go through the time it takes to look up something online when they could just call and get the info in one second over the phone? The reason was that there was something much bigger than my gambling business going on. There was a movement under way—the Internet movement. People were getting hooked on the Internet and wanted to do anything they could on it. It was like playing a game or doing something cool and futuristic, and the demographic of the latter was a pot of gold at the end of the gambling rainbow.

Now I just had to get us there.

DOING BUSINESS ONLINE wasn't easy in the beginning years of the Internet. Those old enough to recall know that, in its infancy, the Internet was slow and the software and services available were primitive. You couldn't run down to your big-box computer store and pick up any kind of software in those days; it was a hardware-driven industry at the time, and the software end of things was only just being developed.

But users of the Internet became loyal, dedicated followers determined to use the World Wide Web for anything they could, even if it meant it would take much longer than a phone call, at least initially.

Demand creates supply, and I knew that the Internet would change everything again, just as going offshore had changed everything when I introduced the first offshore telephone sportsbook to the gambling world.

The Internet bus was about to leave the building, and not only was I going to be on it, but I'd be driving it—or at least deciding where it would go. So I ordered my tech department to prepare to "go live" with Internet wagering no later than March 1, 1998—we had five months to become the first offshore book to take sports bets online. Other companies started offering prehistoric e-mail–driven betting systems before ours. These were very unreliable—and, as it turned out, "trackable" by anyone who hacked their accounts, including "big brother" (the government), which was already adept at intercepting e-mails.

I wanted software that would allow the client a seamless experience and a solid back end. So we went to work designing the ultimate online wagering system. The irony is that even though it never made it "live" to the public (the feds pulled the plug before we launched it), it would wind up being the basis for every sports betting program in existence to this day. So while Costa Rican computer whiz William Ramirez, our software developer, never did cash in on writing the first online sports betting software ever, he will at least get the credit for it now, because he, and he alone, wrote the program under SDB Global's roof from scratch.

IN ADDITION TO all of this, online casinos were on the verge of popping up all over the Internet. To that end, I received a disc from a company called Crypto Logic out of Canada. The disc contained a demo for online casino software—it was incredible. Would people ever play blackjack online? Hell, yes! Let's say it's midnight and you hit your big play earlier on the New York Jets, and you now have three thousand bucks just sitting there in your wagering account because of it. Here are your choices: You can go to sleep, or you can play some blackjack with your winnings. Are you kidding me? I knew this would be a home run for us. No dealers needed, no Nevada gaming license, nothing. It was like a license to steal.

Here's the fax I sent to my business partners back in Brooklyn. (They were so old school, they refused to use e-mail.) This was right after my trip to Canada to demo the casino software from Crypto Logic:

FAX from: SDB Global (Steve Budin)
To: Bo
CC: Donnie
Subject: HOLY SHIT!
   Dear Bo, I just saw an Internet machine that can turn
   air into money! Any interest?
Stevo

I am a loyal guy, and it was only fair to include them, even though I didn't need anyone's investment at that point. Those guys had put me on the map, and they deserved a front-row seat at the greatest show on earth—my show.

SDB GLOBAL WAS making $20 million a year gross—$10 million a year (net) in gambling profits before expenses—at that point. I knew that by adding an online casino and Internet sportsbook by March 1998, I could triple that revenue the following football season with little added expense. "Bo" and "Donnie," my silent New York partners, were like pigs in shit; they knew that they had put their money behind the right guy, and I can't tell you how important that was to me going forward in my life. It was an extra added layer of security that only making money for powerful business-people can earn you. There was a time in Panama, in the very beginning, when I was staying at the Hotel El Panama in the room next to Bo and Donnie. While out on my balcony smoking some sticky weed that I risked my life smuggling into Panama, I overheard a conversation between Bo and Donnie through their open terrace door. It was a heated conversation that rose to the level of screaming. Donnie was questioning putting all this money behind some twentysomething know-it-all—*me!*—who would "probably rat us both out in the end." I did everything I could to bite my tongue and not explode into a rant that could have cost me more than just business. I'm glad I kept my mouth shut, because what I heard next from Bo was very revealing. Bo quieted things down with a calm yet assertive tone, shooting back at Donnie with the following:

"Listen to me, you fat fuck. I am not putting our money behind a kid. I am putting our money behind the son of a legend in our business. I am putting our money behind a kid whose efforts have earned us a fortune on the street over the years. I am putting this money behind Davey's kid, and if he is half the man his father is, he will make us twice as much as his old man ever did! You see, Donnie, sometimes when you're betting on horses, you have to consider breeding as a major factor. Let me tell you something about this kid Steve Budin: If he is crazy enough to live in this dump [Panama] and risk his life to make us money, I say we let him!"

Needless to say, these were not nice people. But I was thankful that Bo was behind me, sort of. With the Internet projections I had on my desk, we had come a long way from that balcony in Panama. I figured we were worth about $100 million at that moment, and I already had begun potential sales talks with some European gaming companies; Victor Chandler was the most interested of the bunch. So I guess Bo did back the right horse, proper breeding and all.

While readying my staff and systems for the March launch of our new online sportsbook and casino, I was simultaneously fixated on how I could drive enough traffic to the site to really take advantage of the serious investment I was making in this Internet technology.

• • •

JACKSON HARRIS WAS a good buddy of mine. We were both from Long Island and lived parallel lives, but we didn't actually meet until we both moved to Florida.

Jackson Harris, Sandy Berger, and I made up the main cast of the "Three Stooges" on Miami's South Beach streets for many years prior to my move offshore. We all used to hang out and hunt out willing females in legendary South Beach dives like the Chili Pepper, Façade, Liquid, and Roses. Harris was a trusted ally; we bonded after I took him into my home during his nervous breakdown. He was suffering from major depression caused by the fear of facing the real world and working. We were twenty-two at that time, so it was a normal thing for most guys our age to go through. I, on the other hand, was making tons of cash as a street bookie and spending it even faster, so I had other issues—if you know what I mean. Harris was a really smart kid who bounced back quickly and took a job with the NBA that he ultimately parlayed into a job with Sportsline USA, an Internet start-up company in the early heyday of multimillion-dollar Internet start-ups. I remained his trusted life adviser throughout his entire rise from low man on the totem pole at the NBA to head of sales and significant stockholder for what would become CBS's SportslineUSA.com, the largest and most heavily trafficked sports information site on the Web in its era and before ESPN had developed a high-traffic website. At the time, SportslineUSA.com had it all: news, scores, weather, odds, and gambling-related analysis. I was Harris's biggest advertiser at the time, spending in excess of $50,000 a month on advertising SDB Global. Spending that kind of dough for online marketing was a first, but aside from porn, gambling was the only business that seemed to be working on the Internet. All other e-commerce models faced serious delivery issues—hence all of their projections of ten years until profitability.

Keep in mind, we were advertising a phone number on our Internet banners, and only at the end of our association was I even offering online sign-ups. Our Internet page was more of an online brochure. That was the extent of what the Internet could offer at the time, because the Web was still almost entirely nontransactional. All of that was about to change, however, and I knew it. People's confidence started to grow as they began to trade stocks online, view their bank account activity online, and buy books online at Jeff Bezos's Amazon.com. This really helped create the demand and ultimately the trust in online transaction-based experiences. While the traffic I was sucking out of SportslineUSA.com was significant enough to justify the $600,000 I was paying it annually, that figure paled in comparison to the $250,000 a month media budget we were executing across all other media (television, radio, and print). There was nowhere else to spend our money at the time, since legitimate sports media companies like ESPN were anti-gaming, owing to their league affiliations (with the National Football League, Major League Baseball, the National Basketball Association, and, at the time, the National Hockey League). With my boy Harris running things at SportsLine USA, this was never an issue—though without him there, we probably would have been shut out there as well.

One day I got a call from Harris on my "Bat phone" in my private office. This was an emergency-only phone that everyone knew not to call me on with a false alarm. He was frantic, and I could barely understand him. Sportsline USA owned what would turn out to be the most valuable URL in the industry, www.sportsbook.com. A sportsbook is a betting house;

gamblers searching online for information about sportsbooks could easily access this URL, and this was what made it so valuable. SportslineUSA.com owned sportsbook.com and needed to make a deal to get rid of it immediately for outward, and inward, appearances.

Understand this: sportsbook.com is the *ultimate* web address in our business. Without even trying, the owner of this URL gets the most visited sports betting website on the Internet. It is the home run of all home runs, and Harris knew it. He was a little prick when it came to negotiations, and I didn't want to risk losing the deal, so I said to him, "Look, after all we have been through and everything, don't take me down a long winding road here. Just tell me the bottom line and skip the sales bullshit—we both know what this means here."

"A one million-dollar flat fee, and it's yours," Harris said. "No negotiations, take it or leave it, and I need to know now."

I couldn't believe he wanted a decision on the spot. Not that I didn't know it was a great deal—because it was—but I was schooled in the art of negotiation, and I wanted at least a chance to counteroffer.

"What's the freaking rush over here?" I asked. "We're talking a million bucks. Isn't that a whole lot of scratch to be asking for a decision in five fucking minutes?"

He explained to me that they were about to announce a sale of their company to a major network—which turned out to be CBS—and that the network, which televised all kinds of sports at the time, including Major League Baseball, college football, and the NFL, could not own any gambling-related websites. So he had to dump the website before the announcement. I asked how this would affect our advertising, and he said that they had planned around the sale by creating an alternative Vegas-themed website that would be able to accommodate all of the sportsbook advertisers going forward.

"So what's it going to be, Stevo?" Harris was hounding me for an answer, and I was sweating and thinking fast.

"Buddy, you want to sell a website for a million dollars to a gambling company? Are you completely nuts?" I asked. "Do you know how many red flags that will raise with the Justice Department?"

The phone went dead silent. I think I heard the shit hitting his drawers.

"You're right," he said.

He asked me for my advice, like he had done his whole life. The wheels had already been turning in my head.

I said, "What if I pay you a million dollars for unlimited advertising, and you just give me the URL for free? This way you get to put the million on your bottom line as a company before the sale, plus you will personally get a onetime twenty percent sales commission on the million-dollar advertising deal." This way the deal wouldn't look like a million-dollar sale of an Internet URL and raise a bunch of red flags. It would look like an advertising deal instead.

Even though the URL was worth every penny, the highest amount ever paid for an Internet domain was something like $50,000. With the advertising tie-in to the sportsbook.com domain sale, I knew it would be a great deal for us because we would receive blanket coverage for one year on the top Internet website for the $1 million—double our previous year's budget, but we would now own and advertise the best possible brand on the market, www.Sportsbook.com. At $1 million, it was a steal for me. Harris didn't know it, but it would have been a steal at $10 million—which is only a fraction of what it went for when it was sold a few years later for hundreds of millions.

Harris loved my idea and said that he would get back to me as soon as possible. I needed to reach out to my partners in Brooklyn to get authorization; while I could certainly pull the trigger on an advertising deal without talking to Bo and Donnie, I couldn't spend $1 million of their money without clearing it first and expect to live to tell about it. This would be the deal of a lifetime, and I was determined to close it. So, like my father taught me, I put it on the yellow legal pad on my desk at the top of my to-do list. This is what it looked like:

1. Clear sportsbook.com deal with Bo and Donnie, and close deal with www.SportslineUSA.com ASAP.
2. Prepare $1,000,000 bank wire for immediate transfer. GET IT DONE!!!

What I was feeling in that moment was akin to what I imagine kings must have felt like when they got a lifetime appointment to the throne. I had been the leader, the creator of offshore gambling, and had paved the path for the others who rode my coattails. I had turned a sleazy street-based business into a respectable international industry that demanded the attention of Wall Street and private investors throughout the world. I had parlayed a couple of million into tens of millions and was worth nearly a hundred million at that point. Hundreds of millions more were on the *immediate* horizon—hell, $1 billion was on the horizon, especially with our plans to move our operation to the Internet. Even with the move online, we'd still have VIP telephone clerks to take "whale" bets of at least a "dime" ($1,000) because those transactions needed to be handled over the phone anyway. We'd also keep the two hundred clerks to handle hundred-dollar wagers and up from customers who simply preferred to bet over the phone, but all of the customers who bet less than a hundred could now play with us over the Internet rather than get turned down because of a lack of phone lines. I was dealing to three thousand players over the phone, and the Internet could turn that number into at least thirty thousand instantly.

I dream big. I always have. And I've always reached the top. But this was Olympus, and the air was thin, intoxicating. The top of the mountain was in sight and within my grasp, with no one in my path and no one in view behind me. SDB Global was about to conquer the world again, only this time it would be ten times over, and maybe a hundred times more spectacular and lucrative.

I drew in a deep breath. All was not well, because as fate kicked destiny in the balls and turned and ran the other way, all the other shit hit the fan. I went from taking off at a sprint in the most exciting race of my life to limping back home, wondering all the while just where that nasty smell was coming from.

MY UNCLE PHIL, a former newspaper publisher in New York City and my dad's brother in every way imaginable, did our Internet marketing out of his old Wall Street commodities office.

Phil put up all the money for our Internet advertising and executed all the deals in exchange for 20 percent of the entire Internet business; this was a nice little cash cow to start off with for Uncle Phil. But he was no dummy. He could see the writing on the wall, and that writing included a lot of zeroes at the end of huge checks. We were all banking on the idea that the

Internet—after a modest launch as the public struggled to wrap its mind around the idea of what it could become—would eventually reach the stratosphere, and we were dead on.

Any customer who signed up on the Internet with us, whether through Phil's efforts or by osmosis, was credited to Phil. Understand, I hated marketing costs: They can really screw up a bottom line for investors. I learned from my days at Caesar's Palace working as a junket rep (which is nothing but a sports betting agent with a really bad commission scale) that the best way to get new customers is via commission-based marketing deals. So rather than piss into the wind, I'd rather they follow a pied piper who knew the route rather than me, because I wasn't going to gamble on advertising. My entire marketing budget was always funded by more-than-willing marketing agents who covered the globe converting players for me in exchange for 20 to 25 percent of the pie their referrals generated.

So our marketing motto was simple: "We pay for profit, period." This really worked because it allowed us to overspend on technology and customer services and ultimately to deliver that polished dream to the end user that we pitched so heavily in the fancy brochures we mailed out by the tens of thousands across the United States.

THE FIRST SIGN that the U.S. government was looking at us came when two men in suits showed up at Uncle Phil's Wall Street office, posing as potential clients.

This was bizarre from the onset. First off, no one ever showed up there for anything. The address was not advertised anywhere, and it was in an office building, not a storefront. The gentlemen came in and said they wanted to sign up for an account with SDB Global. Phil's secretary, Anna, told them that this was a marketing office and that they could sign up only over the phone directly with the Costa Rican operation. They were pressing her for information about the owners and operators, and she became a little nervous about who they were, why they were there, and what they wanted. Phil was playing pinball (his favorite pastime) down the block, so she called Costa Rica and made what turned out to be the fatal mistake of putting these guys on the line with Sandy Berger, my best friend and GM.

Sandy, thinking this was a sales opportunity, and bored with the decreased overall need for any hands-on participation, went into full pitch about the company. He gave out his name, his status as a lawyer (which he was very proud of), even his Florida bar number. Holy shit. He gave his title and his full assurance that their betting experience would be the most professional and enjoyable there was. Just as Sandy got done with what would become his "confession" statement and hung up, Uncle Phil walked back into the office in New York, having received a 911 beep from his secretary, who was sweating bullets already.

He took one look at the two guys and asked his secretary in front of them, "What do these cops want?" One of the men laughed it off and said, "Cops! We're not cops, we're gamblers!" Phil was no moron; he had done it all and seen it all. He asked the guys what they wanted, and they said that they were interested in opening an account, but that they already had all the info they came for and were on their way out. As soon as they left, Phil turned to his secretary and said, "You didn't tell those jerk-offs anything, did you?" She explained that she put them on the phone with Sandy and that they spoke for ten minutes but Sandy did all the talking. The guy was "just writing things on a pad" the entire time.

Phil exploded. "Get Sandy on the line!" By the time Phil got done with Sandy, he was all but convinced that he had just implicated himself in whatever investigation was obviously under way. All of Sandy's greatest fears were coming to fruition. He worked so hard to sign these guys up that it was almost like he was working for the prosecution. He was sick to his stomach and came running into my office in a panic. We called Paul Pringles, our security guy, and sent him to meet with his girlfriend, who was on vacation in the Caribbean at the time. Sandy attended that meeting because I needed proof that this "Cookie" even existed. In that meeting, Pringles's girlfriend once again gave her personal assurance that there was no offshore bookmaking case being investigated and suggested that it might be a local or state police investigation.

What Cookie didn't know was that the FBI's newly formed Computer Crimes Division, originally created to track perverts online, had begun investigating SDB Global and a handful of small-fish Internet bookies, too. Like today, there was no communication between divisions within the FBI in those days. The Organized Crime Division, which had handled every bookmaking case that ever came through the FBI, was all of a sudden out of the loop. Thanks to me, for the first time ever, bookmaking had evolved into a "computer crime," not an "organized crime." So Cookie never thought to check with the Computer Crimes Division. Thanks, Cookie! Love ya, babe!

Or did she? Was Pringles in on it, too? If so, it was the greatest bluff ever, because Pringles knew what cards we had on the table. We will never really know the truth. Personally, I believe neither she nor Pringles knew anything, because Pringles had pocketed so much cash from me and knew his six-figure pay-day was about to evolve to seven if we made it through the next few months and years.

Regardless, without knowing about the Computer Crimes Division, Sandy came back with good news from Pringles and Cookie: There was no federal investigation under way or ongoing pertaining to the offshore gambling industry. So I shifted my focus back to the pursuit of bookmaking greatness and the transition from telephone betting to Internet betting.

IN MARCH 1998, I was closing in on a launch date for the beta version of my first online betting software, and my casino launch was only weeks away. I could feel the excitement in the air, and I knew we were about to take this to a whole new level. All I had to do was lock up the deal for the Sportsbook.com URL, and I was all set. I took the call from Jackson Harris that we were all eagerly anticipating and learned that the blockbuster media deal with Sportsline USA had been approved for the $1 million, along with the transfer of the URL Sportsbook.com.

We got it!

We were so excited that we threw a huge party to celebrate the news. That party lasted two days, as it fell over a weekend. My wife, Melisse, had just given birth in January to our second daughter, Juliette, and was in Miami at the time. So, needless to say, we partied pretty hard that weekend.

Whoever thought that it would wind up being our going-away party? Who would have suspected that the biggest celebration of our lives was actually a wake in disguise?

Monday morning rolled around, and I was at my Escazu estate in the suburban hills of San José, Costa Rica. I was in my private spa facility attached to my garden-and-pool area. I was just sitting in the steam room relaxing, thinking about how best to explain to Bo and Donnie about this new million-dollar marketing deal that I'd just committed their money to. *You won't have to explain a thing,* I thought to myself. *This thing sells itself. A million is a drop in the bucket compared to the tens of millions that will rain down because of this.*

What I didn't know was that the hand I was using to pat myself on the back was about to slap me in the face.

As I relaxed again in the steam room the following morning, there was a knock on the door. My office was on the line, requesting to patch in an "emergency" call from my sister Robin in Miami.

THERE WERE NO emergencies in Costa Rica—especially not at seven in the morning, not after I had just finished swimming laps in the pool at my ten-thousand-square-foot hacienda in the rolling green hills of Escazu. On the agenda that day was the pricing of Learjets so that I could get to Miami and back faster and easier to see my wife and daughters.

What emergency? I thought.

I immediately thought of what I believed would have been the worst possible news. I thought my dad had passed away. He was a sixty-five-year-old armored tank who looked like he was about forty-five, but he had a weak heart from a minor heart attack he had suffered fifteen years earlier. I remember that the two minutes it took the office to connect the call was the longest 120 seconds of my life. I was extremely nervous. I got Robin on the phone, and I said, "Is Dad alive?" to which she said, "Dad's health is perfect. Call Mom. Now."

My other initial thought was that my parents had found out I smoked pot—isn't that crazy? I was forming this speech in my head about how "I'm twenty-eight years old, and I'm about to be a billion-dollar player, so leave me alone with the pot speech, okay?"

My mother answered the phone. She's a redheaded firecracker of a woman, a Brooklyn girl all the way—really. A cross between the mother from *Everybody Loves Raymond* and Andrew Dice Clay, she rules the roost.

"The FBI was just here," she said. "They took your father away." She was in total hysterics.

"What did they arrest him for?" I asked.

"What the fuck do you think?" she yelled. "You've got to call the lawyers."

I had no sooner hung up the phone than my secretary put through a second call to me. It was a reporter from Reuters who wanted a comment, but I thought it was my secretary on the phone, not Reuters.

"The FBI has just lodged a complaint naming you in federal court for Internet gambling," she said. "Do you have a comment?"

"Really? We don't take bets on the Internet," I said. And that was absolutely true—at the time we hadn't taken a single bet online. Little did I realize I had just given the reporter a comment, not my secretary.

Twenty minutes later, I realized how the Internet defines "real time" when I received a call from one of our lawyers.

"What in the hell are you giving quotes to Reuters for—are you out of your mind?" the lawyer, Sam Rabin, asked.

The Reuters story was already appearing on the Internet, complete with my "comment." We were not transactional online—*yet.* In a few days that would've changed. In reality, the law they used to pinch us with was the old "wire act," which specifically mentions telephone betting. The Internet had nothing to do with my arrest. The feds nabbed us in the nick of time because we were ready to blow up the Internet, taking all kinds of bets and running the first online casinos.

"Let me get back to you later," Rabin said. "I have to deal with your dad first."

My next call was to Pringles, our former FBI agent who was making big money as my security adviser—and let's face it, I was only paying him to get me inside information on what the FBI was doing.

"What the hell's going on?" I asked.

"I have no idea," Pringles said.

We got his girlfriend, Cookie, an active FBI agent, on the phone.

"I just found out there's a new division, Computer Crimes," she said very apologetically. "I never knew about it—until now."

She said she felt very bad, and she sounded upset; either she really was, or it was just a great performance. Pringles wasn't happy either, as his future life as a millionaire in Central America was done, and he'd be headed back to the States to live off his meager government pension.

"Listen," Cookie said. "Whatever you do, I recommend you surrender immediately. Don't make a mountain out of a molehill. With where we are with the case now, you aren't going to be in a lot of trouble unless you make yourself a fugitive. Be the first to surrender and make a good deal for coming back first."

That was what my lawyer had told me minutes earlier. My lawyers negotiated my surrender, and I was told we'd earn some "good faith" points by doing that.

I later learned that this was part of a much larger bust. All the bookmakers who had followed me south and were using both the system and the software we had developed were hit—the

"Internet 21" we were dubbed by the media. Some were in Costa Rica, and others operated in Curaçao, the Dominican Republic, Antigua, and other island countries. Many told the feds to go screw themselves and went right on with their business as if it were just an annoying phone call. A half-dozen remain fugitives to this day. Some, I believe, honestly thought they were facing hard federal time: Federal sentences are served in full, with no time shortening for good behavior. Others knew the feds couldn't come get them because the local governments in these countries valued the jobs—and technology—that the gambling operations brought in for local workers. And a few knew what we were on to with the Internet and knew that even though they'd never in a million years get the billion-dollar payday we were leaving on the table, they could still make millions, probably even multimillions (it would turn out to be tens of millions even for smaller operations) once betting came online.

Here's how the 1998 prosecution broke down. Of the twenty-one Americans charged by the U.S. Justice Department with breaking the Federal Wire Act by using a "wire transmission" facility to accept bets on sport, Jay Cohen got the longest sentence: twenty-one months in prison, but just a $5,000 fine. He was found guilty on all charges he faced, and he was the only one of us who fought the charges in court. Rumor has it that Jay spent time in a Las Vegas federal pen, and it turned out to be a real pain in the ass for him, if you know what I mean. Poor Jay. Five others surrendered and didn't contest the felony charges (including my dad); three (including Sandy) turned themselves in and pleaded guilty to charges reduced to misdemeanors in plea deals; four surrendered but had the charges dismissed (including me, but I accepted a huge fine); and seven remain listed as fugitives. One of the more notable defendants still on the run is Steve Schillinger, an options trader from San Francisco who co-owned the telephone and then online sportsbook World Sports Exchange (WSEX) in Antigua. Before he started WSEX, he resigned his membership in the Pacific Stock Exchange after exchange officials questioned him about bookmaking on the exchange floor.

Whatever I wound up selling my company for was nothing compared to what it would have fetched had I had the time or notion to sell to one of the European gambling companies, which operate to this day with licenses from their own governments.

The end result is a net loss to the U.S. government, because guys like me made between $10 million and $20 million a year and paid 37 to 40 percent U.S. taxes, thus making the U.S. government our full partners on every dollar of profit we made. By putting me out of business, that money was gone, as it was for the other U.S. offshore-based bookmakers. That money went straight into the pockets of the foreign countries that then took over and operated our businesses—and about nine out of every ten dollars still comes from U.S. bettors to this day. That's the kind of mind-set that has weakened the U.S. dollar against the euro. We've got economic problems in the United States exactly because of decisions like these.

HERE'S HOW IT broke down that morning prior to my mother's call. At 6:30 AM local time, the FBI showed up at my dad's house in Miami with guns drawn and fingers on the triggers. The government stages these spectacular "raids" when they want to play to the media. They arrested my father and charged him with conspiracy to commit bookmaking in violation of the Federal Wire Act.

My dad had had nothing to do with the operation for over a year by that point. Because the FBI couldn't have gone to Costa Rica and arrested me for doing something that is legal in Costa Rica, they snatched my dad instead and used him as the bait to get me to close up shop and return to face charges without a fight.

Robin was distraught, and my mother was a mess. My mom thought she had put the horrible memories of my dad's run-ins with the law behind her for good—only to see their door busted in and my dad taken away in handcuffs. To make things worse, my wife Melisse was dealing with postpartum depression after giving birth to Juliette. She had just arrived in Costa Rica after not seeing me for a long time—and was greeted with this news. She was devastated. She was scared for me and concerned about the future of our family.

I immediately got on the phone with our lawyers to try to bail my father out, but the feds falsely labeled him a "flight risk" to force me to agree in writing to close my company and return as part of his bail agreement.

Clever move by the FBI—there is no winning when you go up against them. Even if you are in the right, the best you can ever hope for is a draw via submission. All you can try to do is minimize your loss. So I wasn't even afforded the opportunity to defend myself in court and save the business. Instead, with no chance to explain my position, they forced me to close SDB Global. The FBI knew I would not allow my dad to sit in jail while a trial went on for months, maybe years. I wanted my dad out on bail that day. So I went from taking a steam and contemplating the hundreds of millions that the new Sportsbook.com domain and SportslineUSA.com deal would bring in, to agreeing to immediately shut down my business and return to the United States to surrender to the FBI. What a swing of events. There had been two outs in the ninth inning, and I had a full count on the batter, but I had to forfeit the game and declare it "game over."

I went to the office immediately to start to wind things down and strategize with my lawyers.

The first thing I did was make sure *every* customer got their money sent to them via FedEx or UPS. That was important to me. I came into the business and built a reputation based on honesty and never owing anyone a dime. I left it the same way. Everyone got their money again, just like before, when we shut down the office in Panama and moved to Costa Rica. I remain proud of that fact.

I learned that news travels fast even in the remote outpost of Costa Rica, because I was met by a special delegation of lawyers and diplomats bringing a message from the president of Costa Rica, Jose Figueres—and a Costa Rican citizenship application. The message was that I could stay in Costa Rica and avoid U.S. prosecution; the caveat was that I could no longer return to the United States—ever. I couldn't live with that—I love my country.

So while that was a tempting offer, I couldn't let my dad sit in that cell indefinitely. The fact that the FBI knew that—which was exactly why they grabbed my dad in the first place—makes me question whether Pringles and his girlfriend were in on it.

That was a brilliant chess move by America's "finest"—forget the terrorists plotting against our country, they had Steve Budin to fry—but there was nothing I could do but accept the checkmate like a man and surrender.

I was done and I knew it.

For the first time I had run out of options, answers, and fixes. Game over.

JACKSON HARRIS ENDED up doing the exact same deal (of which I was the architect) and sold Sportsbook.com to a front group backed by an Irish kid nicknamed Purple. I couldn't resent Jackson for that. What was he supposed to do? I was finished and he knew it.

Purple was operating a tiny Internet sportsbook out of the Caribbean at the time. He was struggling to keep his fledgling eleven-man operation afloat, working all day and sleeping under his desk at night.

But Purple raised the million dollars he needed and paid it to Jackson Harris's company, Sportsline USA, for the Sportsbook.com URL and unlimited advertising—my deal to the letter. Sportsbook.com recently sold for about $200 million; the company is publicly traded and worth about $1 billion right now.

You would have thought that the U.S. Justice Department's declaration of war against offshore bookmaking would have put SportslineUSA.com in a precarious position. Yet under the protective banner of the First Amendment to the U.S. Constitution, SportslineUSA.com became the biggest facilitator of sports betting on the Internet via its offshoot Vegas-themed website, which marketed various Sportsbook companies (for a tremendous fee) and drove tens of thousands of clients to bet. While I knew all of these things were going on behind the scenes, I never brought them up to the feds. I'm not a rat, and I was unwilling to deal any information in exchange for help. Besides, I'm a bookmaker, not a murderer. What was I ever going to be facing vis-à-vis jail time? Nothing!

I was focused on the business at hand, namely, getting my father freed and keeping us all out of prison. So I returned to the United States to face the music. I was booked into a New York City federal prison by the U.S. marshals.

What a bunch of animals they were.

Believe it or not, I had never been to jail before, and I was nervous, to say the least, even though I tried my best not to show it. I was handled separately from my dad and didn't see him at all throughout the entire time I was booked and processed.

I was led to my cell at the end of a mentally exhausting experience, only to be met by my dad in the cell.

We embraced immediately, and I remember crying—not sobbing, not weeping, but lightly tearing. Oddly enough, those weren't tears of sorrow; they were more of a relieved expression of joy. Without having to verbalize it, we both knew that regardless of where we were at that moment, we were together. We also knew that together we had accomplished so much over the years—most of which we had spent the last two days saying good-bye to.

Our accomplishments were so far beyond what we originally set out to do that regardless of the unfortunate situation we found ourselves in, we couldn't help but be proud of what we had done.

We were modern-day pirates, pioneers, and bookmaking visionaries.

We were rock stars.

Despite it all, he told me, he couldn't have been more proud of me, and that meant more to me than any stinking jail cell we were in.

He was and is my father, my best friend, my mentor, and my hero. All I ever wanted to do was earn his respect.

He used to say when I was a kid and I'd question him: "Why do you question me? Aren't I always right? Have I ever been wrong? Have you ever been right?" So ever since I was a little boy, I always wanted to be right one day. As bad as our surroundings were, I was finally right, respected, and acknowledged by him in a way that I had been seeking for as long as I could remember, and it was a strangely wonderful coming-of-age moment for me.

WE SPENT THE night in jail together talking about it all and trying to get some closure.

I was really surprised to find out that my dad felt responsible for the outcome by having brought me into the business at a young age.

I was also surprised to hear that he was relieved that the charges were so, as he called them, "insignificant."

He had feared that the ultimate outcome of our offshore endeavors would be much worse than it was. But I had no regrets, and by the end of the night, he knew that.

We were both mad at the U.S. government, though. We felt betrayed. We paid all of our taxes—which was an easy way for them to track me—making the U.S. government our 37 percent partner, and they treated us like criminals, even though paying taxes and never laundering a single cent of money showed that we wanted to remain aboveboard, or at least wait until the same U.S. government defined the gray area in which we operated.

But deep down, my dad was happy to finally close the book on everything gray, and he was anxious to live out the remainder of his years in black and white.

I told the prosecutor that all he was doing by arresting me was sending my ten thousand customers looking for another book. He snapped back, "We're going to get a few easy guilty pleas, and then the rest of them will fall like dominoes."

I just smiled and thought to myself, *Bullshit, dominoes.* I knew that all the veteran European bookmakers were jumping into the game now and that the United States could never arrest European owners. What were they going to do? Invade London and arrest legal, licensed bookmakers? Bookmakers are like stockbrokers in Europe. It would be World War III if the U.S. government even tried. I knew that at that point the feds had no idea what they were doing other than stopping me and those who had followed the rainbow and caught the overflow from the pot of gold I'd discovered.

I knew that because of the extreme demand SDB Global had created, they would never stop this business. It was like trying to enforce Prohibition. In the poker game of the business world, demand trumps all cards. By arresting all the taxpaying Americans in the business, like me, all they did was make sure that zero revenue (by way of taxes) came back to the United States.

Brilliant.

One of my lawyers was Aaron Marcu, a 1980 Harvard Law School grad who had been a federal prosecutor for seven years before he went into private practice. Having him represent us really helped. But the government wanted to make its stand. U.S. Attorney Daniel Becker stood up and said, "The federal government is not in the business of selling off prosecution. You can't buy your freedom here."

Nobody said a word. Aaron told us to leave the room. He finessed the deal for my father, and then the charges against me were dismissed as long as I paid a hefty fine. Because I had paid taxes and never laundered money, I signed a plea deal and the U.S. government's attorneys agreed to a few million dollars in fines and an admission of guilt. But while in the grand scheme of things the fines weren't catastrophic, the federal iceberg had still sunk my $100 million company like the *Titanic*.

I SOLD MY company's remaining assets in a fire sale for as much as I could, and the proceeds covered all my legal fees and fines. In the last few days when I was winding down the business and closing up shop, my dear friend and head of customer service at the time, P-Man, approached me with an offer from his two cousins in Greece to buy the company's assets, equipment, etc. It was my last chance to make a score before closing, so I did it.

P-Man and his cousins opened up the following year as SBG Global instead of SDB Global, and they have been running ever since without so much as a peep out of the U.S. government. I assume that's because the company is now a foreign-owned company, so what can really be done?

Sometimes my experience has seemed like "selective" prosecution: It was like everyone was allowed to mine for gold in the gold-filled mountains I discovered except for me.

I spent most of the following year avoiding prosecution by fulfilling my pretrial obligations, which included staying above the law, gray areas included. My dad, bless his heart, stepped up like the man he is and pleaded guilty to a felony—in connection with a company he had absolutely zero involvement with at the time—so that Sandy Berger would walk without one. Otherwise, Sandy's telephone confession to the FBI in that final week of our business would have certainly earned him a felony charge and disbarment.

My dad went before the judge and was ready to do time for Sandy. You see, prior to Sandy taking the job with me, his father, Marcos, an old-school Brooklynite like my dad, asked to meet with my father to get his assurances that Sandy would not be in any danger. He didn't want to hear it from me—the guy loved me, but he also knew I could sell ice to the Eskimos. My dad sat down with Marcos, looked him in the eye, and promised him that he would never let Sandy get hurt. That was all Marcos needed to hear. He and my dad spoke the same language, and it didn't require many fancy words. So my dad was merely keeping the promise he had made to Sandy's dad—a natural decision for him, and one for which Sandy is forever grateful.

In fact, the judge recommended house arrest for my dad, and my dad replied, "Your Honor, please, you don't know my wife—anything but house arrest! I've been on house arrest for forty years. Give me the hole, just not house arrest, I beg of you."

The judge smiled and fought to hold back laughter while everyone else there cracked up—except the prosecution, who were realizing that their huge, airtight prosecution had turned into a farce. They had fried the biggest fish, only to let the biggest bounty of all off the hook forever. They'd never have a chance at netting that fish, much less getting it to pay U.S. taxes—as we had done and would have continued to do.

My dad was a sponsor of the Paralyzed Veterans' Organization and one of its top contributors; he had dedicated almost all of his free time and extra funds to champion that cause and many other worthy causes over a twelve-year period. My father was always teaching me, mostly by example. I was a willing student and always watched his every move. He taught me that a tough son of a bitch you wouldn't want to fuck with could also be a grateful, spiritual person, and generous to those less fortunate, all without ever sacrificing his edge.

The federal judge reviewed my dad's distinguished charitable record, considered the victimless crime, and reduced the suggested prison time to house arrest and probation, despite my dad's joking pleas for hard time. My father had several arrests on his record from when he was younger, and the judge could have hit him between the eyes with the proverbial book. But that was trumped by the man my dad was, and his sentence was better than anyone could have imagined considering all the effort the feds had put into busting us.

I wound up with a deferred prosecution for four months, but one of the conditions was drug testing. I had never been a drinker, and I never was into the hard drugs like cocaine or meth, but I did use pot—often, and a lot. In fact, I took a bigger risk getting good pot out of the United States and into Costa Rica than I faced running an offshore bookmaking operation.

So I found myself off pot for the first time since high school graduation. Let me just say for the record that I don't want to glorify marijuana or any other drug. I used pot because it relaxed me after the sixteen- to eighteen-hour sprint-marathon days I put into building and running a high-adrenaline business. The pot kept me sane. That might sound like a pathetic attempt to justify the way I used pot as a "medical" marijuana use, but it is what it is. And sorting through all the emotional baggage as I awaited sentencing was not easy, especially without the weed. I had lost so much: even more than my income stream I had lost my purpose and my passion—my power, my ego, and my built-in excuse to act however I wanted, and without fear of any repercussions.

I was building my dream home in Miami as all of this unfolded. Sitting in the backyard of my new home, I was as miserable and low as I had ever been, grieving from the losses. I not only had to figure out what to do with myself now but, even more than that, figure out who I was.

As I sat there, I watched my beautiful wife Melisse, who is nothing short of a goddess—long dark hair, beautiful brown eyes, and big curvy lips that you could park your Harley on. Beyond her penetrating physical beauty is the soul of an angel. She stuck by me through it all: Panama, Costa Rica, and even jail. I realized finally that my bitterness and "woe is me" attitude were getting me nowhere. I have always been a God-fearing man who relies heavily on faith. Looking back, I believe that God saved me from myself by getting me out of the business and out of Costa Rica. Though at first I had looked at getting busted and losing my business as a curse, I was beginning to see it, through divine intervention, for what it really was—the biggest blessing of my entire life.

All of the events of the past few years crystallized in one powerful moment when it suddenly hit me: While I was busy trying to build my billion-dollar company, one customer at a time, I had lost focus on what was really important in my life— my two kids and my unbelievable wife. I had neglected these angels for four years while expending every ounce of energy trying to become a member of the billionaire boys' club. While I was always able to effectively evaluate the worth of my business at the close of each fiscal day, I had failed to realize the value and worth of being the CEO of my family. So it was only when I was finally stripped of the ego-inflating, high-powered position of building and then running the largest sportsbook in the world that I was able to realize my truly priceless asset— my family. To think: They had been in my portfolio the whole time, but I just didn't see them and add them to my bottom line. I thank God that my time in Costa Rica was cut short before I reached the point of no return and lost what was most valuable to me—my family. I was forced to trade billions in future gambling fortunes for the love of my family. Loving them and giving of myself to be loved by them is, to be honest, the best deal I ever made.

So I got up off my sorry ass and went back to life with a new, reborn spirit and determination. Only now I vowed never to lose focus on what was most important: my family and my God. Life is good.

2

Bookmaking Beginnings

Bookmaking was the family business, and I got my start as a student at North Miami Beach High School. My father was a bookmaker, and I wasn't involved in his business—yet. I had come from a family of bookmakers, so I had grown up around it. And I was very aware of what was going on with my father's work. We'd go to the Bahamas when I was sixteen, and I'd play advanced craps games, understanding very early on every aspect of the game. I had a knack for numbers and betting strategies. My father couldn't help but be proud of the fact that at sixteen years old, I knew every bet denomination and payoff on the craps table. Every wise bet and every sucker bet.

In addition I had a very aggressive money management system that came from always playing with Pop's money. I mean, realistically, all casino games are sucker bets. I remember sitting upstairs in my dad's suite after a giant craps hand in Vegas when he broke it all down to me. He was always teaching me before, during, and after a significant experience. I remember hitting a craps hand with my dad for 180k when I was sixteen at Caesars Palace in Las Vegas. Nobody worked a crowd at a craps table like my dad. He had a crowd about twenty deep around the whole table, a hundred people in all, watching his every move, hypnotized by his frenzy as he unleashed his quantum craps karma to the tune of thirteen points (the point is the number the shooter is trying to make) and 180k. If you're doing your math at home, we bought in with about $1,500 in cash and cashed out with $180,000. It was a big score. He was ranting, raving, willing each point in, and playing the crowd like John McEnroe at the Wimbledon finals. Serving up winner after winner, he was throwing the dice all the way up to the ceiling—always prompting a canned response from the pit boss: "Mr. B., keep the dice eye level for me, okay?" My father would reply, "Yes, sir, very sorry about that," then turn to me and wink. The next throw would bounce off the chandelier, a good thirty feet above the craps table. At the very height of the hand—the very pinnacle of the moment—we needed a six to win about $50,000. A hard six would bring us in about $100,000. It would be our thirteenth pass. My dad looked around at the screaming crowd, which by this time was worked into a foaming rage by the pure adrenaline of this craps hand, and raised his hands to bring everyone to a complete dead silence, like an NFL quarterback on a Monday night home game, just before coming under center.

Holding the dice in his hands, he waited until there was absolute quiet, not a peep, everyone shushing everyone else to get them quiet and then leaning in to get a view of the table. My dad then whispered to me, in the still of the moment, "What number is Patrick Ewing?" Then he whipped the dice around the table so hard that they both came all the way back to our side of the table. I thought quick and hard about what number Ewing was and as soon as I remembered I yelled it out:

"Thirty-three!" I looked down in front of us, and laid out on the felt by our pass line bet were the two dice, three-three. The crowd exploded in a roar. Sheer pandemonium.

I never saw so much money and so many chips in my life. My dad was like a craps god, and the whole casino was worshiping him. Nobody more so than me. He was my hero, the man I knew I wanted to be exactly like.

The next events were equally impressive and important, and typical Dave Budin. After hitting the hard six and the big payoff, he took all his bets down without ever crapping out or even establishing a fourteenth point. The crowd, especially at the table, was dumbfounded. They just couldn't believe that he was walking with the chips and not continuing to press the hot hand. They started shouting at him to please shoot again. He just smiled and said, "What goes up must come down, and there is no honor in sinking with the ship, gentlemen."

When my dad spoke to fellow gamblers at a crap table, it was like Gandhi addressing a peace conference in India. Everybody hung on his every word and rallied around all of his statements. As fast as the crowd had gathered to watch this amazing show of gambling prowess, they dispersed just as quickly when the show was over. We went back to the suite, and he gave me my share of the winnings: ninety thousand bucks. Can you believe it? I was sixteen years old at the time; it was like a million dollars to me.

However, the speech my dad gave me along with the money was worth more than millions to me. That night my dad explained to me that the only way to win consistently at gambling was to *be* the house. He explained that if I was going to continue gambling my whole life, it didn't matter how much I won on one hand—I would eventually lose everything. So I asked him: How was I ever going to become the house? How was I going to buy my own casino?

"Maybe one day, son," he said, and then he pulled a parlay card from the sportsbook out of his back pocket and set me on the path to becoming the house. Parlay cards can be broken down into different kinds of prizes: picking four- and five-team parlays, or five- to ten-team parlays. He showed me how I could pass these parlay cards out to all my friends in school for $10 each and completely clean up. It was like stealing: With a parlay card, a bettor picks every game on the card by penciling in who he thinks will win against the spread (how many points a team is predicted to win by), which is set up by bookmakers. Say the Giants are playing the Jets. Well, maybe the Giants are really good this year, so just about anyone would pick them to win. But if the spread is fourteen points, the bettor has to decide if the Giants are that good—if they can win by more than fourteen points. So it's not as simple as picking the winning team. The "line" (the spread) changes throughout the week leading up to the game. If the big money is coming in on the Giants "covering"—winning by more than fourteen points—then the line goes up even more, so that gamblers will get to the point where the Jets are a good bet. Or if the betting is heavy on the Jets—meaning that bettors think the Jets could lose by thirteen or fewer points, or even win the game—then the line moves to thirteen or twelve points to encourage more bettors on the Giants.

On the parlay cards, the bettor has to "hit" (pick correctly against the spread) every game to win. For example: To win $10,000, the bettor has to put down $100 and has to hit every game. People always say, "I knew the Giants would win," or "I knew the Raiders would beat the Bills," but to bet against the spread and get all the games right on a given weekend is almost impossible. Still, the rush that bettors get from thinking they know something other people don't drives them to bet. Again, again, and again. If they are wrong, they want to make up for it the next week. And in the following weeks. They almost never win, though. Even if a guy gets lucky and picks the right teams once, he gets cocky and the next week bets more and loses all the money he won. He's betting more because he's gotten some confidence and thinks he's better than he really is. It's a vicious cycle, and one that eats up bettors' money and lines the pockets of the bookmaker. Sometimes the worst thing that can happen to a struggling bettor is hitting big, because the vision of what he could win expands and he thinks the betting world is at his feet—but soon he's at its mercy.

When I was in high school, a lot of my friends and teachers bought parlay cards from me, and that eventually led to parents and friends of parents buying them, too. This was small-time bookmaking, usually only $5 and $10 parlays. Naturally, the cards came from my father, so I kicked back some money to him. The bettors would have to pick all the games correctly to win, and in two years I collected a lot of money and rarely paid out a dime because in this game there usually were no winners. Correct that: I was the only real winner, thanks to my dad's sound advice and direction on that historic crap night in Vegas.

By the time I was a senior in high school, my business had grown. My friends' fathers were now betting big-time through me. As their bets got bigger, I started hooking them up directly with my father, because the parlay cards weren't sufficient for these "dime" ($1,000) and up players. Most adults bet on games (not parlay cards) with my father over the phone, since all bets $50 or higher were handled over the phone.

As an "agent," I got a percentage of what they bet. An agent is someone who brings bettors to a bookmaker. And as an agent, I was second to none.

In sports betting, the bookmaker always makes more than he loses. But I was throwing away money as fast as it came in. A teacher I had enlisted into my business got really lucky in the middle of football season and hit a parlay card for five grand. Coming off another weekend of fun—blowing the thousands I was making each week—I wasn't in a position to pay out the $5,000. I wasn't thinking tax bunkers or financial plans. I had only one place to go: my father.

"Dad," I said, "I have this situation."

My father gave me the money, and I turned the customer over to him.

As a senior, my other teachers were getting in on the action with the same lack of success as the students. Our high school gym teacher, who was an assistant coach for the football team, became a big bettor with my father. While I recruited these guys and made a nice cut from them, they were my father's clients, since he was the one they trusted to pay them and they feared him too much to ever consider nonpayment. The gym teacher got in the hole in a hurry. He already owed me $800 after just the second week of football season. One day he waved me into his office.

"I have a problem," he said. "But I can get you the money in two weeks."

This teacher was a big guy. I was a tall kid with an athletic build, but I was no gym teacher. Still, he knew about my father, a six-foot-four former college basketball player and legendary New York bookie with a no-nonsense reputation.

So I played good cop/bad cop. I always took the side of the customer (or so they thought), as I did in this case.

"I'm with you, Coach," I told him, "but my dad is an animal."
The teacher nodded his head gravely.

Everyone knew my dad was this big monster in the background waiting to chew anybody up. Coach obviously did not want to get my dad involved in this collection.

"Listen," I told the teacher, "here's what we're going to do."

The gym teacher listened intently. He wanted to pay his debt, but he was hooked at that point and also wanted to keep betting.

"The eight hundred dollars—we're going to make it four hundred dollars," I said. He looked relieved, so I continued. "All I want in return is for you to get some of your teacher friends to start playing."

This was, of course, assumed to be all hush-hush and confidential.

"That," he said, "is no problem."

By the end of the week the gym teacher had gotten five other teachers to start playing. I brought them into the fold, giving them the phone number to my dad's business. That was the best $400 I ever spent on "marketing." I ultimately lowered my coach's credit to $250 a week, and he never got in trouble again. In addition, I was bringing in several more of my friends and their parents. Parlay-card bettors initially, almost all of them invariably ended up becoming bigger bettors with my father over the phone. Between teachers, friends, and their parents, I ended up with fifteen to twenty solid private phone customers, and my business grew exponentially. It was addition by subtraction: By forgiving a $400 debt, I picked up another thousand-plus a week in business.

It's important to note that I wasn't a phony with these people. I wasn't their friend just to get their business—we were friends because we honestly liked each other. Somehow it always turned out that my friends and their parents were the people I ended up doing business with. They trusted me and brought me their money, and out of that money I was getting an agent's cut, roughly 40 percent. Not bad.

The high school kids who were betting weren't your average high school students. These were kids from affluent Aventura in Miami—all of them had trust funds and big bank accounts. Their fathers had a lot of disposable income. I worked up to about thirty guys and was making $5,000 to $10,000 per week from everyone I had hooked up with my father. Needless to say, I wasn't pushing $5 parlay cards anymore. The transition to full-time bookmaking agent had occurred.

Larry Zader, the father of one of my high school friends, was the perfect example of a typical customer. The forty-five-year-old tycoon was a good customer of mine. I remember hanging out with his son Eric one day, as was not uncommon, when Larry came into the room.

"There he is—Stevo!" He welcomed me enthusiastically. "How are you, baby?"

"Never better, Mr. Z.," I answered.

Eric's father looked around the room to make sure no one was around.

"Eric upstairs?" he asked.

"He just went up to crack the books," I answered. "Classes are getting tougher this fall."

"Yeah, he isn't the brightest. Thank God he has my looks and my money," Larry said.

"Amen to that," I replied.

Larry took me into his private office downstairs, set his briefcase on the desk, and pulled out an envelope marked "Stevo, $1,820," and set it on the desk.

"The Dolphins killed me this weekend," Larry said. "If they make that one field goal at the end, just a freakin' thirty-five-yarder, Stevo . . . I mean, come on, it's the NFL, and they're playing in the sunshine. For the love of God!"

"Well, look at it this way," I said. "If you had won, the thrill would be over already. Now you're going to rant and rave about this until the weekend!"

Larry's dad lit a cigarette and inhaled, talking as smoke seeped out of his mouth.

"You wiseass," he laughed. "Hey, don't forget to have your guy drop off some schedules for me."

He wanted a list of upcoming games. He was hooked—win or lose, they all love the action.

"Consider it done," I answered.

Larry handed me the envelope. I didn't need to count it. I knew exactly how much was in the envelope, and even how it was broken down in bills.

"Just keep that warm for me," Larry said, smiling confidently, "because it will be coming back to me next week."

"Sure thing, Mr. Z.," I answered. "I'll even keep it in the same envelope just in case."

Larry nodded at me.

"Seattle's quarterback is hurt this week," he said in a quiet voice, confident he had inside information no one else could possibly have—and thus an inside track not just to getting this money back but winning more. "No way Seattle wins by six at Cincinnati this week if he's out."

"You got it," I said.

"Tell your pop I send my best," he said as he walked me to the door.

"I will," I said.

Larry Zader was worth his weight in gold. He had a $25,000 line of credit and always paid up each week on the button—a dream client. He had a few winning weeks here and there—everybody does—and when he won, I would get his money to him, as I did with anyone else, first thing Monday morning. Bookies in the past took time to pay until after they collected—if they even paid then. Part of the reason we did such good word-of-mouth recruiting was that we always paid up right away, and that reputation was worth millions. When somebody won, it was just "marketing" money to us, because once a guy won, he was sure he could beat the system and he'd wager all he'd won and more the next time. And as rare as it was for someone to hit a parlay, it literally almost never happened two weeks in a row. Even if it did, I'd get back the money times ten the following week as the lucky bettor's false sense of confidence grew.

I was building the business one sucker at a time. I'm not using the term "sucker" derisively—I don't mean to say that the person was a fool or a loser. Suckers are recreational gamblers, regardless of the amount they wager. Larry passed his brother Freddy my way, and he was a huge bettor, dropping $20,000 a game—we called those guys "whales." A couple of whales, and you were golden. Freddy loved betting the favorites, and occasionally he won.

But not more than he lost.

No matter how big or small the gambler is, they all lose in the end. Gamblers bet until they simply cannot afford to any longer. It's a hobby, a passion, for them, not unlike playing the stock market, only in this case they think they really know what they're doing. All sports fans who gamble think they know what they're doing, whether it's the guy playing the weekly pool in the office or in the newspaper or the guy who puts down $10,000 with a bookie. There is no system to winning in sports betting—the majority of all bets are lost. But to the bettor, each bet is an adrenaline outlet that gives him an unequaled rush. It is the "money for nothing and your chicks for free" mentality at its best.

The irony is that losing gives the bettor the bigger high. Winning just gives them more money to bet—and more money to lose. They are addicted to losing because it is a "low" that lasts all week long. Winning is short-lived, a quick high that only sets up the powerfully deep, dark high that is losing. And no bettor ever wins—they all lose, except the bookmaker. To me, that was euphoria like heroin on the first hit, only I won week in and week out. Being a bookie was like being in a special club of people who got to win at gambling—what an honor, what a life.

I was rolling in dough at a very young age, but all of that money was going right out the window. Nothing was too expensive, and no expense was too ridiculous. I impressed my friends by taking them out to strip clubs even though I was way under twenty-one. I had every doorman on my payroll, and the city was my playground. In a way, it was good that I was reckless with my earnings at an early age and got it out of my system, because it could have really hurt me when I made real money years later.

I got a reputation. I'd walk into a club with my friends and there'd be a private table waiting for us. We'd show up outside a packed club and the doorman would let us right in, without having to wait in line. Image was very important, and I was very cognizant of that, which in itself was another important lesson. With my mouthpiece and gift of gab, and my dad's muscle, I was in position to become *the* bookmaker for the discreet affluent clientele who saturated the magic city of Miami. It was my turn to shine, and I hit the gate like Seabiscuit.

3

Betting 101: An Overview

BACK IN THE mid-1980s when I was introduced to bookmaking and sports gambling, there was a big crew out of New York run by two associates of my dad's, "Henry Madman" and "Mitchy Sniffles." These guys were the sharpest gamblers on the East Coast, from sports to gin rummy to poker, and they backed several private card rooms in New York City where big shots would gamble at high-stakes poker and gin rummy. Guys could lose $100,000 in a night playing gin rummy in their joint. They also "backed" bookmaking businesses throughout the United States, including ours. They would back as many sucker businesses as they could, and at the same time they were sharp bettors themselves and would place bets with a hundred different bookies all over the country. They knew all the moves, all the off lines, and they had access to every hot crew and their games. They were betting as much as they were booking and cleaning up on both sides. Bo, who later wound up backing our offshore business, ran the entire "sharp betting" side of Henry and Mitchy's business, and that's how we originally hooked up. When Henry and Mitchy retired, at least publicly, Bo and his partner Donnie, a heavy-set gambling degenerate who also happened to be the sharpest football bettor in the entire country, took over all of their operations for them, and we were backed by Bo and Donnie instead of Henry and Mitch from that day forward.

When I was getting my start in Miami, my dad was actually a betting agent, not a bookmaker anymore. He was a bookmaker his whole life in Brooklyn, New York, but when he moved to Florida, he stopped taking the bets and became a betting agent specializing in accumulating the best sucker customers from across the globe. A betting agent was responsible for bringing customers to a bookie in exchange for a commission on the customers' losses. Agents sent multiple customers to a bookmaker and developed a "sheet"—the list of customers on whom an agent is earning a commission from a bookmaker.

My dad wasn't a typical low-level agent. He ran the entire business, soup to nuts, with me as his eventual point man on all fronts. He ran the bookmaking office, handled the pay-and-collects, and made every decision from small to big. Nobody took a piss without consulting him first. This was not typical for an agent: Usually the agent brought the customer to the bookmaker and the bookie handled the rest. My dad's designation as an agent stemmed only from the simple fact that, from a risk standpoint, he wasn't booking the bets. The risk was being assumed by Brooklyn (Bo and Donnie). My dad didn't trust anyone's people, so he always did everything himself; at the end of the day, he was the best in the world at it, so it was a win-win for Brooklyn. Like I said, this wasn't the norm, but then again, there was nothing normal about us and our way of doing things.

I will now spell out for you the multiple advantages that agents provide to bookmakers. First and foremost, commissioned agents are a great deal for the bookmaker because they bring him tons of business from one solid, verifiable source. The agent represents one contact point for anywhere from twenty to a hundred potential customers, but he's the only one the backers have to trust for the money. Not only is the agent the source for customers, but because he is earning on the deal (as much as 50 percent), he is also the guarantor and therefore fully responsible for all monies owed to the bookmaker from the customers on his sheet. Also, the agent is the only guy who knows the backer's identity, and so not all the customers are calling the backer's office to bet. The only risk the bookmaker takes in this scenario is the risk associated with taking the bets. With the type of suckers we brought to the table over the years, that was about as risky as backing a slot machine. When you run your book correctly, a bookmaking business is just like a slot machine: volume times a percentage equals gross gambling profits.

There are some big misconceptions when it comes to how a bookmaking operation fundamentally works. First, let me lay to rest two of the biggest misconceptions right now.

The biggest misconception is that bookies earn 10 percent on football and basketball. Not true—they get only 5 percent. The origin of this misconception comes from the fact that when you bet $100 on football or basketball, you are risking $110 to win $100. So people figure the bookie is earning 10 percent. This, however, is the way the correct theoretical percentage of the earnings on football and basketball is calculated: profit equals volume times 5 percent.

If two people bet $100 on football or basketball, the most probable mathematical outcome is that one will win and one will lose, since each game (with the point spread) is a fifty-fifty proposition. In this scenario, there is a total volume bet of $200.

If one guy wins, you need to pay him $100. If the other guy loses, you collect $110 from him. That gives you a profit of $10 after paying the $100 and collecting the $110. A profit of $10 on $200 volume is equal to 5 percent.

So bookies are only working on between 5 and 7 percent, as percentages get higher with specialty sucker bets like parlays, teasers, and proposition betting. Even so, straight wagering on football and basketball represents 80 percent of all bets.

The second biggest misconception is that bookmakers "even out" their books by "laying off" action to make sure their books are balanced—hence the name "bookmakers," as in "make the books even." That is the biggest crock of shit I have ever heard in my life. I hear this more than anything else from people who think they know everything and don't know jack shit. That belief is just false.

First of all, this misperception comes from little schoolyard bookmakers and college campus bookies. I am not even talking about these amateurs when I use the word "bookmaker" in this book. They represent a segment of bookmakers who are booking bets on a limited bankroll and who therefore might lay off action if it exceeds the amount of risk they can afford to take on a game. In addition, there is a segment of bookies who work on no bankroll at all; they are total busted-out scammers who have no intention of paying off. These lay-off strategies, although often attempted, never work and usually wind up with the middleman (in this case the underfunded schoolyard bookie) getting a beating from a real bookie for not being able to pay off whatever action he was laying off. Why? Because when his customers slow-pay him or don't pay him at all, he still has to pay the place he laid the bets off to, and we've already established that he doesn't have a bankroll. That equals a beat-down every time. This was why I was so successful. All these half-assed, underfunded idiots were the only option for gamblers in Miami up to that point—that is, they were the only option until I showed up on the scene with a bookmaking bankroll funded by the deep pockets of Bo and Donnie and an operation behind me run by the best in the business, my dad. If bookmaking was cocaine, I had the fucking freebase, and once they tried my shit they could never go back.

The "even-out-the-books" myth also comes from bookmakers telling their customers (who, as in my case, were usually also their friends) that they don't care if they win or lose because they even out their books by laying off the lopsided action and just earning the rake. Bullshit! That's just a way to make your friends feel warm and fuzzy about handing over their loot, week in and week out, until they're broke and you're rich.

So here is the final word on laying off action and evening out the books: If you are properly funded and stocked with the proper customer base, you want to take as much action as possible and you don't care what they bet on or how lopsided the betting on a game is.

A proper customer base does not include "wiseguys," by which I mean sharp bettors, not mob guys or mafioso types. In the sports betting world, the word "wiseguy" refers to a professional gambler, or someone who makes money by gambling on sports. Wiseguys are the 1 percent of the gambling public who actually turn a profit, in most cases by being ahead of the bookie on the information chain. They are getting info on injuries, weather, and, more importantly, the line changes before the bookies do. If you are always laying (-5) on games that wind up (-7), and taking (+10) on games that wind up (+7), you are

a wiseguy and an undesirable client for any bookmaking operation. Like my dad taught me, if you stick to suckers only, you
know at the end of the year that you will earn your 5 to 8 percent on your total volume of wagers. Get your sucker-volume
up and the profit will rise along with it at an equal pace.

My dad said it best when he explained to me: "To give away
volume by laying it off is to give away profit, and that is simply not a Jewish thing."

Suckers are retail customers—customers who bet based on
their gut feeling, not on any significant research, data mining,
or connection to the sports underworld of wiseguys. Suckers
have no access to lines and moves and no connections to Stevie Z, the Computer Kids, the Poker Crew, Billy Walters, the
Israeli Totals Connection, or any other professional betting
crew whose job is to consistently beat the odds and who
always do. Suckers are just normal doctors and lawyers looking to add a little excitement to the game and to get some
money for nothing.

Before I took bookmaking offshore, there were two different types of shops that took sports bets, wiseguy shops and
sucker shops. Wiseguy shops mostly dealt to all the sharpest
bettors, the professional gamblers; they moved the lines very
aggressively and constantly kept the books as close to level as
possible so there would be no room to take chances with such
"wise" money on the line. Because these shops kept their
books very tight, they could not afford a lay-down, so they were
usually run by the type of people who always got paid, if you
know what I mean.

These shops represented 20 percent of all shops out there.
Our shop, like most shops, tried to be a sucker shop. The most
profitable shops, sucker shops, were mostly run by Jews in New

York, not the mob—which is misconception number three: that the sports gambling world is run exclusively by the mob.

Like all sucker shops, we did not deal to any sharp bettors and would chase any bettor who was getting the best of us. Sharp bettors would always try to sneak into our shop, but when we caught them we made sure they never wanted to come back.

Before I started the offshore sportsbook business, a large betting office usually had about nine guys. The head bookmaker set the lines and reported back directly to the owner. He usually had eight clerks working the phones taking bets from between one hundred and five hundred bettors on a Sunday. Every phone had a cassette tape recorder hooked up to it— nothing high-tech, just a small Radio Shack device. The recording was to be used in the case of a claim—someone saying they had won when in fact they had lost—and there were always plenty of claims. It is amazing how many people swear they bet the Nets until they hear the tape of themselves saying, "Gimme the Knicks," and they are sincerely amazed.

I remember a conversation my dad and I were having with one of our biggest customers, Steve Schwartz, a Merrill Lynch VP. He made a few million a year in the commodities racket. He told us that sometimes clients would deny that they ordered a sale or a stock purchase to avoid paying the loss. He said the best they could do was blacklist a claimer, but they couldn't collect if there was no proof. My dad convinced him to put in tape recorders, like he did for our claims. It was the early '80s when Schwartz installed his first tape recorder at the New York offices of Merrill Lynch, and eventually every single firm on Wall Street installed the machines. So you can really credit that innovation to my dad.

To effectively run a bookmaking office, you needed one guy to get the betting-line changes out to each clerk and help the head bookmaker manage the individual credit limits of each bettor in real time. Credit limits changed daily as clients went in and out of the good graces of their agents, who were ultimately on the hook with the bookie for all losses. Agents would call in before each session started and give the head bookie a fresh list of updated credits for all of their customers. This was in the days before computers, so all of this info was recorded on worksheets, copied on copy machines, and passed out to each clerk for use during the betting session. And yes, these credit calls from the agents were also taped, just in case the agent himself caught a case of amnesia and didn't remember authorizing his customer to lose $50,000, money the agent would be on the hook for if his client bailed.

Before I took bookmaking offshore, all shops ran on credit systems. In that pre-computer era, every bet was written by hand on three-carbon paper. Two different people could then use the extra copies to score the tickets at the end of the day and compare results for accuracy. The third copies—"the pinks"—were hidden in a secure underground trapbox in case the place got busted. The cops would confiscate all the tickets, but would never find the pink ones. This third copy was crucial, because the day after a bust a bookmaker could be very vulnerable to false claims. While everyone who won would have their figure ready, people who lost weren't about to admit it absent of proof.

Busts and pinches were a normal part of the business and only affected the clerks in the bookmaking office. The owners and bosses were never there to get pinched; they were in payphone communication with the head clerk from remote locations to get all the updates. For this reason, every shop had a backup office with phones already hooked up so that in case of a bust they could go back to work the next day. For a long time in New York (most shops were located in Brooklyn and Manhattan) these busts were all misdemeanors and you were out the next day. Whether you had twelve arrests or forty didn't matter much if you weren't applying for a normal job anyway. Then New York, under Rudy Giuliani, changed bookmaking to a felony that could be reduced to a misdemeanor, and that changed everything. At that point, second offenses became a mandatory felony and led to jail time. When this happened, most people opened up shops in Philadelphia, where to this day bookmaking laws are the most lenient in the country. Philly is now the top choice for most ex–New York bookmaking shops that can't afford another bust.

Clearly, there were a ton of pieces that needed to come together for a bookmaking business to work, and all those pieces needed to be kept as quiet as possible to avoid attracting the law. You needed an office with clerks to write the bets and grade the bets. You needed a separate crew to pay and collect from the customers. You needed agents to bring in the business and a front man to talk to the customers and pretend he was the boss as an extra layer of protection for the real boss. All these elements had to work in sync, and needless to say, there were some good organizations and some shitty ones. I always felt we offered the best overall operation on the street back then because of how we fused all of these services and functions together and presented them to the end user as one solid organization with flawless execution.

I always looked at being a bookmaker as having a license to steal. It was a privilege and an honor. It is no wonder that in places like London and Australia bookmakers are looked at like stockbrokers and considered well-respected members of the business community. To be a good bookmaker you must be honorable (always paying what you owe) and fair (in how you treat your customers). For example, if I have a guy who calls every week and bets every favorite on the board and never bets an underdog, what do I do? Here are the choices: (1) deal him half a point to a point high on all favorites—he will never know, and we will earn 15 percent more over time—or (2) deal him the real line. A good bookmaker will overlook the 15 percent short-term gain and protect his integrity so that he will have the best chance to retain all of his clients for the long term.

I was constantly dealing with slow payers and customers getting jammed up. Credit is a big part of the business. Before I went offshore and began to require that customers post up their money, bookmaking was a 99 percent credit business. This is by far the hardest part of the business from a management perspective, and this was also my specialty on the street. There were two schools of thought on credit. The mob-backed tough-guy shops would purposely give their customers five times the credit they merited and hope that they couldn't pay. Then they would have these customers pay points to their "in-house" shy-lock forever, and the 10k that the customers originally owed would cost them ten times that before they finally got it paid off. Bookmaking wasn't the real business, but just a tool to get customers over to the real business, which was shylocking: paying points on a debt that was just paper money anyway.

While this was certainly a clever scheme, it didn't appeal to my mentality; I was a bookie, not a loan shark. In fact, we gave clients less credit than they deserved, because we knew in advance that no matter how much we gave them, they would need a little extra on a Sunday night. We always gave guys a little extra room on Sunday night, so why give them more than they could pay? Keeping credit low was the only way to stay away from headaches because *nobody* likes to pay after they lose, absolutely nobody.

I wasn't a gangster, but it was important that my customers fear repercussions, without feeling threatened to the point of not wanting to do business at all. Remember, we were dealing with respectable members of the community. This was a fine line that I mastered walking. It certainly helped to have my dad, a legend and true Brooklyn tough guy, in the background. I was able to play good cop/bad cop with him whenever I needed to get respect without taking the heat directly and damaging my daily relationship with a client. This allowed me to form bonds with all my clients, since I always appeared to be acting on their behalf whenever a situation arose. At the end, I wasn't even asking my dad what to do, just pretending to go back to him for a judgment. I was in my very early twenties, so people needed to think that they were dealing with my dad. I always made them aware of where we were coming from. They realized quickly that no disrespect would ever be tolerated by our organization.

All of this did not completely prevent problems. We had customers who would simply lose more than they could afford to, and we would arrange payment plans (interest-free) and allow them to post up additional money to play while they were paying off an old debt. My dad would always say, "Look, son, they are going to play somewhere. It might as well be with us."

Certain guys were multiple offenders, and they were ultimately pardoned and made into complete cash (post-up) players. By that time, after multiple credit offenses, they knew one thing: that we were honorable, even though they had proven not to be. So they would rather post up funds with us, and continue to play, while they took credit from and screwed other bookies.

You can't just throw away guys who love to gamble because they are not good payers. You have to give them a post-up place to play in while they are getting into trouble everywhere else. Very few, if any, bookmakers were equipped to truly handle post-up clients. First of all, I offered post-up clients seven-day-a-week delivery and pickup service and had a staff of drivers ready to be dispatched 24/7. If a post-up client called at 7:30 Sunday night to post 10k, we were on the way like Domino's—there within thirty minutes to pick up. If the bettor won, we would deliver the winnings the next business day. That was service, especially in a town where many bookies didn't pay at all.

We were the first to proactively and successfully train problem payers by turning them into post-up players and eliminating the risk completely. We turned undesirables into VIP clients; as post-up clients, they were treated like fucking gold because they had gone from being high risks to literally money in the bank. My dad took the biggest negative in the business and made it work for us. Those are some of the things that separated him—and eventually me—from the other street-level bookies, who weren't delivering the same level of service we were. We brought an "out of the box" business mind to the otherwise street-level craft of bookmaking. Even before offshore books, my customers always felt like they were doing business with a real company, and they were.

Here is how our original roster looked on paper.

I was running the business and talking to every customer on

the front end while bringing in new customers and attracting agents to bring their business in.

The Pittman brothers, Jeb and Dirk, distant cousins on my dad's side, handled all the pay-and-collects, seven days a week, for post-up clients and credit customers. Jeb looked like an overweight six-foot-four version of Jack Black, only minus the education, talent, and humor. Dirk resembled Hutch from the '70s show *Starsky and Hutch*. They ultimately disappeared— after $300,000 in cash was mysteriously stolen from a lockbox that only they had access to. We knew where they went to hide in north Florida, but we never went after them because they left behind a house that my family had given them. The house was a wedding present to Dirk, but it was in my father's name for mortgage purposes. The house was worth 300k when he gave it to Dirk, and 750k after the four years had gone by. So with the house's appreciation and Dirk never planning to return, it turned out well for us. They weren't the smartest guys—they both left school at a young age—but my dad had a thing for hiring family. He was a loyal guy who had made a deathbed promise to his uncle Sol (their grandfather) to take care of the Pittman brothers.

Tony Russo was the head clerk in the Brooklyn office, where the bets were taken. Tony was a perfect match for this position. All the guys who worked as clerks were his friends and followed his direction. He was very smart and knew how to talk through problems on the phone with clients and sound authoritative yet respectful. He was also very honest and trustworthy. He would later become like a second son to my father and a brother to me. He was on the front line and in the most vulnerable position. There were many nights when the cops broke down that office door and Tony would be taken off to sit in jail while my life went on unimpeded and uninterrupted miles away from the problems that he faced for me. He ultimately moved to Vegas and retired. We are very close to this day, and he is the godfather of my son Jace. Tony grew up in Bay Ridge, Brooklyn, and some of his many close friends there ultimately went in a very different direction from him. Tony always afforded us the benefit of his association and friendships with some of the most respected guys in Brooklyn without ever allowing any of these contacts to come back to haunt us in any way. There was no doubt that he was the true muscle behind us on the street, and he knew how to use it for everything it was worth in our equation.

My father, Dave, was the master, a black belt of the seventh degree. Fuck that, he was a ninja! He made every decision and watched over his entire operation. He was a better clerk than Tony or anyone else we had. A former math teacher, he was a better figure man than our figure men. He was a better decision-maker than I could ever be, and as tough and strong as the animals Tony knew and associated with in Brooklyn. My father was, quite honestly, smarter than all of us put together. He ruled with an iron fist and settled for nothing less than perfection. He was a teacher, always teaching me and everyone else in our crew. He was an expert's expert and would get calls from all over the country from top bookmakers in need of advice and clarification on certain rules. He was the authority on all bookmaking issues. Guys like Bobby Martin, who ran the infamous Churchill Downs sportsbook in Las Vegas, would get my dad on the phone when he needed to ask a question. Legends like Davey Goldberg from St. Louis, a notorious East Coast bookie who later ran the sportsbook at the Dunes, was another person who would contact my dad from time to time with questions like: Did you hear anything on the street about a certain game that moved five points, and was it a betting crew or just a bunch of suckers on the same side? My dad had the inside info on every move, and the best of the best would always make sure that his number was in their Rolodex for one reason or another. He knew things that nobody else knew.

In addition to being tough, he was extremely deep. Bookmaking was just a mirror of real-life strategy for him. So when he was teaching me how to be the best bookmaker I could be, he was really teaching me how to be the best person I could be, morally, ethically, and spiritually. He made me into a sharp, long-term strategist at an early age. He made me a thinker by challenging me to think and by always allowing me to make mistakes in order to find my way. He always wanted the best for me, but he knew that he could only give me the best of what he had to offer, and that turned out to be a heck of a lot. To this very day, he always defends me, right or wrong, and gives me unconditional love and strength. He is a true leader who teaches by example. He never asks me to do anything that he isn't willing to do himself, and he's never met a task that he wouldn't rather do himself. He was and is a huge success, as both a father and a bookmaker.

Bookmaking was a way of life to us. We loved what we did, and we did it better than anyone else in the world. Delivering a product that felt entertaining while consistently costing our clients thousands each week was an art form, and I was fuckin' Pablo Picasso, baby, suckling wisdom from Michelangelo.

While my dad was incredibly book-smart, his real education came from the streets. He'd go to high school for a few hours a day, then go play pool in the neighborhood pool hall. He eventually learned to be quite a hustler and was making a lot of money playing pool. He also learned how to play cards—poker and the most popular New York card game among gamblers at the time, gin rummy. It wasn't my father's math acumen that helped him become one of the greatest poker and gin rummy players in the world—arguably the very best during the time he played. When it came to playing cards, he was more like David Blaine than Doyle Brunson. My dad was a magician with a deck of cards. This is called being a "card mechanic," and he was one of the best. Don't get me wrong, he was a great overall player, too, and he never tricked everyone. However, if someone was trying to cheat him, he always made sure he got the last laugh—and the best laugh, too. Furthermore, if the kids needed to eat and the rent was due, he made sure he always brought it home, by any means necessary. There was no winning when he was dealing, and that became a metaphor for his life.

But bookmaking was where he would really shine, and fueled by a game that he didn't have to cheat at to win, he embraced a new path and direction and never hustled cards or did anything unethical again. He respected the privilege it was to be a bookmaker and never again tempted the gambling gods by hustling easy marks on the side.

My dad was invited to London, England, for a private poker game sponsored by a famous aristocratic country club in 1958. He was twenty-five years old. This seven-man game included some of the wealthiest young poker players in the world. My father showed up, and the game was already going. He noticed right away that all the cards were marked. He could spot these things a mile away because he was a professional and because he never met a deck of cards that he couldn't mark himself. They were using two types of decks, red and blue, and going through three to five marked decks an hour.

My father then went to work on these card-marking amateurs.

He slowly and methodically stole a red and blue used deck off the table where the discarded cards were sitting. It took him about an hour to get the two decks into his possession and tucked away in his pants. When he had the two decks secured and the time was right, he excused himself to go to the restroom, where he proceeded to preset the cards in a perfect order. This is called "preparing to put in a cold deck." He prearranged the hands so that each player would think he had a great hand and bet everything he had in the pot-limit-style game that they were playing in—and then lose it all to my dad's hand, exactly how he prearranged it.

This move was extra difficult in games where cards were marked. My dad was six-foot-four and could palm a basketball. It was easy for him to hide his cards in his huge hands so that nobody saw the markings on the cards. Then, when it was his turn to deal, he switched the decks out and put in his cold deck. Sounds easy, but he was working in front of a live audience with no net. This was no piece of cake, but for a seasoned talent with iron balls like my dad, it was a walk in the park. Once his deck was in play and he was dealing, he knew who would get what exactly, what they'd ask for—everything. He was a magician with a deck. He knew how to cut and mix the deck without moving a card. Nothing moved no matter how many times he shuffled or cut the cards. The guy to his right had the traditional last cut, and my dad took his half like it was going on top, but it went right back on bottom. After the big show of shuffling and cutting, not a card had changed position. All these well-to-do guys from Europe and all over the world tried to run a high-stakes hustle, and my dad robbed them blind. He robbed the robbers—he loved that—and he took $1.4 million for his time and effort.

He started working with some of the biggest bookmakers around, including Gil Beckley out of Cincinnati, who was king of that part of the country. He had another top connection to Eugene Nolan, who was out of New Orleans. These were "wiseguys," who, as previously explained, have extra inside information and know who is likely to win. A wiseguy sets lines and sometimes fixes games.

Just before becoming a bookmaker, my father was a "mover"—he moved money for powerful wiseguys all over the country. These guys trusted my father. He'd also make his own bets on the side. He had the street credibility and the backing to do whatever he wanted. He knew how to bet on both sides of the line to guarantee he'd make money whether his team won or lost. Since he was almost never using his own money, he really cashed in.

At one point in his early years, my father had a $100,000 debt he was supposed to pay a bookmaker. He was broke and desperate, so he didn't pay and instead relied on his street connections to bail him out. As a result, the mob put a hit out on him. In fact, the hit man was the notorious Colombo soldier, Joey Gallo. But my dad was as crazy as anyone and had the same kind of connections the mobsters did.

The way these situations were handled was with a "sit-down": His mob guy sat down with Joey's. My dad's connection immediately went to bat for him, and the dialogue was classic.

"You don't understand," he said. "Davey's been with us for

years. His job is to rob bookies. We have people that rob jewelry stores, nightclubs. Dave's job is to rob bookies and kick back to us. He makes a living from robbing bookmakers and kicking up to us, and we can't let you stop a guy from making a living."

Classic. What can you say to that? This wasn't a mob bookie he beat; it was just a bookie who reached out to the mob to help him collect his debt from my dad. A debt that became uncollectible. The mob guys backing my dad really liked him. Of course, they liked most the fact that he was good and reliable and made them a lot of money by getting tons of money down on all the hot games for them. In effect, he got his operating license from them. That's how things work on the streets.

I guess you could say that in order to evolve into the bookmaking legend he eventually became, my dad had to travel the dark, winding road he did. If you don't want to get cheated, you must know how to cheat. If you don't want to get muscled, you have got to have muscle behind you. These were all necessary evils and par for the course when it came to street-level businesses like bookmaking. He had to always be one step ahead of everyone, including the law. He had to be wiser than the wiseguys.

After successfully transitioning from street hustling—doing what he had to do to survive—to successful bookmaking on the street, my dad never stopped reminding me of the stark differences between the two. He was always teaching me, always telling it to me like it really was. He started talking to me like a man when I was very young, and I think it made me think and act like a man, even as a teen. He knew he had to prepare me for the game, and he wanted to be sure that he gave me everything he could before he made his exit from the business.

My father taught me the single most important thing that kept me out of trouble: Never, under any circumstances, cheat the U.S. government out of its end of anything. To my dad, kicking up to the U.S. government via taxes was just the price you paid to play and no different than kicking up to the mob bosses who ran the streets. Always pay taxes, he told me, and never launder money. My father and I can both proudly say that we've always paid taxes on everything we've made. He was a math whiz and did his own taxes, but when I started my business, the first thing I did was hire the best team of criminal lawyers, accountants, and tax attorneys I could find to keep me safe within the gray area I was operating in. I'm an American, and Americans pay taxes. So I paid my share. That's ultimately why I got arrested for bookmaking, not tax evasion. I paid all my taxes and therefore never had to worry about ever doing any significant time in prison. And once again, it was a lesson taught to me by my father.

MY FATHER ALSO moved money for a legendary guy named J.R., who worked with the mob in the Midwest and ran the biggest bookmaking office in the country at that time. J.R.'s big hustle was fixing games. He'd take bets and then adjust the line accordingly so that bettors would put their money on the team J.R. knew was going to lose in the fix. Then he'd turn around and actually bet on the games he was fixing to get a double bang. My dad would get big bets down for J.R. in return for a fee and in order to always have the inside information from J.R. and the fellas, the sharpest betting crew in the country. He never knew what was going on with J.R.'s fixes. In his business of moving money, there was a strict "hear no evil, speak no evil" policy. Besides, when you're dealing with mob guys, there are

some things you just don't want to know. Because of his connections on the streets of New York, my dad moved big money
with amazing results and made J.R. and his organization a lot
of money. This is why even someone like Joey Gallo ultimately was convinced to back off from whacking my father: he
was just too important to too many heavyweights.

The most famous J.R. fix was the 1954 Oklahoma–Oklahoma State game in the midst of the Sooners' forty-seven-game
winning streak, one of the most dominant runs in college football history.

J.R. and his crew in Chicago had been using my dad like so
many others did—to move money on hot games that they
wanted to bet big dollars on. My dad got a call from J.R. on
Monday morning and heard him say something he had never
said before: "Dave, bet us as much as you can on Oklahoma
State this Saturday, at *any* number, and make sure you bet it
early because I don't know how long it is going to stay on the
board."

For J.R. not to specify an amount to my dad was unprece-
dented in their relationship. This was serious, and my dad knew
it. He got down for a heap of money for J.R.—and himself, too—
without knowing what J.R. had done or had "going" on the
game, but figuring it was as close to a sure thing as there was.

My dad never knew what the people he moved for were
doing—he just knew that whatever they bet on always seemed
to win, so he followed them and always cleaned up. By Thursday stories hit the newspaper about OU players getting mysteriously sick, and sure enough, the game was taken off the board
and betting was suspended for two days, just like J.R. had said.

Betting resumed on Saturday, game day, along with the
announcement that OU would play without more than a dozen

key players. My dad read the papers and was furious. He felt used and betrayed. He had moved money for game fixers in the past, but he'd never signed on to move money for people who poisoned athletes. My dad called J.R. on it.

"What the fuck is this in the papers?" my father demanded.

"Take it easy, Dave. We do what we do, we don't check with you for permission," J.R. asserted. "We pay you to get our action down, end of story!"

My dad understood the type of people these were and wasn't going to take it any further than that. There was silence on the line for about two minutes, then J.R.'s cocky voice shot back.

"Don't you want to know the story, Davey?" J.R. asked enthusiastically. "It's a good one!"

"Shoot," my dad said, eager to find out what really went down, and J.R. couldn't wait to tell him. He went right into the story without hesitation.

"We got ahold of this colorless, tasteless, odorless liquid laxative for horses," J.R. said. "Supposedly just one spoonful would leave a man shitting his pants within minutes."

By this point he had the full attention of my dad, who couldn't believe what he was hearing.

"I wanted to be sure this stuff worked before we used it, so we had Tony Fingers test it for us in a bar in Coney Island," J.R. said. "While some innocent jerk-off went to the bathroom, Fingers put the stuff in his beer. As soon as the guy came back from the toilet, he took a swig of the beer."

Tony Fingers got his nickname from having only three fingers on his right hand.

"Tony told me," J.R. continued, "that within thirty seconds the guy looked left, looked right, and then shit his brains out into his pants, eventually sliding completely under the fucking table and into the freaking fetal position."

J.R. let out a few belly laughs from time to time; he was really amused with himself and the story. He then brought himself back from laughing and continued to tell my dad what they did.

"I sent my guys out to the hotel where the Sooner players were staying before the game," J.R. said.

The betting was heavy that week, with Oklahoma favored by twenty points to win over their in-state rivals from Stillwater. That meant OU had to win by twenty-one to cover. The goal was to get Oklahoma to win by fewer then twenty-one points. No one cared if OSU actually won or not—the Sooners just needed to be slowed down so that Oklahoma State could cover the spread.

J.R.'s voice started to build to a steady pace as he related the story step by step.

"I sent Fingers into the hotel kitchen through a back door, and he grabbed a cook and brought him outside where nobody could hear or see them talk," J.R. explained. "He wound up slapping him around and scaring the shit out of him. Nobody likes to get bitch-slapped by a three-fingered hand, you know what I mean, Davey?"

A full belly laugh and a pause came next, then right back into the story.

"We gave the cook a few hundred for his pocket and the laxative. The cook poured the laxative into the soup, and all but about fifteen players enjoyed a hearty bowl of spiked soup, about thirty-seven players in all," J.R. said. "These guys were literally falling on the floor, crapping in their pants right at the tables, because they couldn't get to a bathroom. They shit for three days straight, Davey, three fucking days!"

The newspaper reported that the players were taken to the hospital and that no one ever figured out what it was, even though three dozen healthy football players were having this severe problem. In those days, players often played both offense and defense, but with fewer than twenty healthy guys who hadn't eaten the soup, the Sooners weren't sure, until game day, that they could even play. Betting on the game was postponed a couple of days, but everyone who was in on the fix had already bet the game earlier in the week. Betting resumed on Saturday when the Sooners decided to play with a depleted roster. The Sooners still won the game, but the final score was just 14–0. J.R. and his crew made a killing as usual, and my dad did pretty good himself.

My dad never moved money for J.R. and his crew again. He was really disturbed that the guys he was moving for would do something like that, thought they reportedly repeated the same feat five years later in Chicago, when Oklahoma visited Northwestern. My dad was a college ballplayer at that time, and he felt that giving players a horse laxative was crossing the line. He was lucky to have walked away from J.R. and his Midwest crew when they later got into a heap of trouble with the law. In the game my dad played, knowing when to walk away was sometimes the key to winning—or at least to staying free to play another day.

The stories my dad enjoyed telling me the most were the double con–like situations where a game was supposed to be fixed but wasn't—a true double sting. One of the better stories involved New York University and its star player, Cal Ramsay. First, some background.

My father was doing some business with the notorious game fixer and former NBA rookie of the year, Jack Molinas (who later did federal time for game fixing). Molinas had been a straight-A student at Columbia before he was rookie of the year at Fort Wayne, which drafted him in the first round of the NBA draft with the fourth overall pick. Molinas also grew up with my father in the pool halls of Brooklyn, so they had hustled together before. Molinas's brother would later write a book about Jack, but my father knew things that even Molinas's brother never knew, and he has never divulged them.

Until now.

Molinas was suspended from the NBA in 1954 for fixing games, but he was still doing it even though he no longer played. Molinas was plugged in with a high-roller wiseguy named Joey Hacken, who was sponsoring all of Molinas's work at that time.

My dad was looking to raise some capital at the time, so he hatched a plan to take advantage of the greedy Molinas and his sponsor Hacken, who always screwed everyone over and had no respect or regard for the codes of the game. Hustling the hustler was my dad's forte at the time. He was like a cross between Robin Hood and Paul Newman in *The Sting*.

He called Molinas and met him for coffee. My dad told Molinas he had three guys on a local college team, and he wanted to get them some money to fix games: Cal Ramsay, another standout named Cunningham, and a nonstarter. He also had a fourth guy who didn't play on the team but was the ringleader of the crew. Molinas asked to meet directly with Ramsay. My dad said he couldn't do that because Ramsey had too much to lose, but he could send over the ringleader. Problem was, my dad didn't have one player, much less three or four, on the NYU team, or any other team for that matter. So he went to his father-in-law's factory, where they put labels on steel files, and talked to a tall African American named Jamal, a hard worker who had worked in the factory for several years. He told Jamal what the plan was and offered him $500 to help out and disguise himself as Ramsey's friend and the ringleader of this crew of game-fixing NYU players. He told Jamal to sit with Hacken during the games and to be sure to wear sneakers just in case things went bad and he had to make a run for it.

My dad counted on Jack Molinas to be the same backstabbing cocksucker he'd always been. That's why he was hustling him in the first place. My dad told Jamal in advance, "Listen, Jamal, the first thing that scumbag Molinas is going to do is try to cut me out of the deal so he can earn my piece on top of his."

My dad instructed Jamal to make sure that he went along with it and agreed to cut my dad out. My dad knew that this would later absolve him of any involvement in the hustle, and that was exactly his plan. He also knew that as soon as Hacken met Jamal, Hacken would look to cut Molinas out of the deal, and that would make my dad twice removed and untouchable in this heist.

My dad got Jamal a pair of top-of-the-line Chuck Taylor Converse high-tops, and they went to meet with Molinas. About halfway through the meeting, my dad went to the bathroom. While he was in the bathroom, Molinas propositioned Jamal to cut my dad out completely so they both could earn more. Well prepared for this, Jamal gave Molinas his telephone number and agreed to discuss it in full detail later, when my dad was not around. Four days later, my dad got a call from Molinas saying that Hacken was going to pass on the deal. This was obviously bullshit: Molinas was going forward with Jamal and without my dad, just as planned.

Molinas immediately set up a meeting with Joey Hacken and Jamal. Jamal told Joey that the "contract" was for $12,000 per game, with each player getting $3,000 and Jamal taking $3,000 himself. Jamal and Joey exchanged telephone numbers, and Joey told Jamal to expect his call and answer the very next day. Hacken loved the deal, but he felt he needed more proof that Ramsey was really in on this. Hacken called Jamal the next day and said that he had to at least see Cal Ramsay's jersey—Jamal would have to actually get it and hand it to Hacken. That would legitimize the deal.

Jamal told my father this, so my father called up Cal Ramsay, who would later go on to play in the NBA before becoming the New York Knicks' TV announcer.

"Cal, it's Dave," my dad said. Cal knew my father because my father had recently been a standout player on the Brooklyn College basketball team and was well known locally. "Cal, I just hate to bother you, but there are these kids with leukemia in the hospital. Cal, they were breaking my heart, and I told them I'd do anything they asked. One of them said, 'All I want is to touch Cal Ramsay's jersey.' Now, Cal, can I send Jamal over to pick it up? He'll get it back to you the same day, I promise you that."

Ramsay was almost in tears. He agreed to meet with Jamal and give him the jersey. Ramsey gave him the jersey in a brown satchel. Jamal took it to Hacken immediately. Hacken took one look at the satchel and told Jamal, "That's okay, you don't have to take it out, I believe you. You are here, you obviously have the jersey. I don't even need to see it."

He took it out anyway. Hacken was hooked.

But Hacken didn't want to pay Molinas a cut of this deal, so he told Molinas that he was going to pass on it. Meanwhile, after seeing the jersey, Hacken went forward with Jamal, exactly as my dad planned it. My dad was now twice removed, and facing no risk. Jamal promptly returned the jersey to Ramsay. Remember, this was back in the 1950s before teams licensed their apparel, and so there weren't team jerseys for sale in stores anywhere.

The next night Ramsay and his teammates started a streak that would go zero-for-five against the spread, totally looking like Jamal had actually paid these guys to dump the games—even though neither Ramsay nor his teammates ever knew a thing about it! Jamal sat next to Hacken each game, with his new sneakers on and one foot in the aisle, ready to run if NYU pulled away at any point.

Hacken went five-for-five and made $100,000, and my dad made $12,000, less the $500 he paid Jamal. When the players graduated, the Knicks drafted Ramsay. Shortly thereafter, Ramsay was in Vegas shooting craps at the Dunes, and who should happen to spot him? Joey Hacken. A short guy from the old neighborhood, Hacken went up to Ramsey at the craps table, patted him on the back, and motioned him to bend down so he could tell him something in his ear.

"Hey, I'm Joey Hacken, the one who paid you to dump the five games last season. Good work."

Ramsay backed up. "What the fuck are you talking about?"

"Those five games at NYU—I bankrolled that," Hacken said incredulously.

"Man, I have no idea who you are," Ramsay answered.

"Cal, you sent me your jersey—your game jersey that you gave to that guy to show me!" Hacken pleaded.

Obviously a faint recollection of loaning his jersey—to my father, not to this crazy Hacken guy standing in front of him—crossed Cal Ramsay's mind.

"I never gave my jersey to anyone ever except for the one time I loaned it to Davey Budin for that sick kid in the hospital," Ramsay said.

My father's home phone rang minutes after this interaction.

"I tip my hat to you, Dave, you slick cocksucker," Hacken said. "You are the very best, my friend."

My dad fired back: "I don't know what the fuck you're talking about, Joey. You and I haven't been friends since your boy Molinas cut me out of that deal with NYU, so fuck you and fuck that thief Molinas, too!"

Later Molinas and Hacken would each get five years for fixing more than one hundred games.

Molinas's personal story had an even worse ending. He screwed a lot of people and nearly ruined the career of Connie Hawkins, who was slated to be the Michael Jordan of his era. For just knowing Molinas, Hawkins was kicked off the basketball team at the University of Iowa and then blackballed by the NBA until he was twenty-seven years old. Hawkins's first year in the NBA was 1969, and he promptly made the NBA all-star team. Though Hawkins's career was still impressive and culminated with induction into the Basketball Hall of Fame, there's no doubt that he could have been one of the greatest of all time had he been able to finish his college career and begin his pro career on time.

After Molinas did his time for fixing games, he came out ready to hustle. The pornography industry was just getting started in New York, but since Molinas's name was dirt there, he went to California and bought a movie house that was closing down and turned it into a porn theater. In California at that time the mob controlled the porn industry. Like the garbage business is run by the mob—just because nobody admits it doesn't make it any less true. Molinas's porn house was cranking out a profit right away, so the local California crew called Molinas in for a sit-down after about two weeks of business.

"This is our game," they informed Molinas. "You can't work here. You will have to walk away from the operation, and we're taking it over."

Molinas then rolled the dice a final time, and while it paid off in the short term, it would turn out to be the kiss of death for him. He name-dropped a New York boss's name.

"They told me if I have any problems here in Cali, to just mention their name," Molinas said in his best—and final—sales pitch.

"You are with New York?" they asked him. "Well, that changes everything. You can stay, but you still have to pay us. Let's say twenty percent gets kicked up to us, and consider that our final offer."

Molinas gambled and won, or did he?

Almost two years later the boss from New York was invited to a big "family" wedding in L.A.

"Hey, I did you a real solid," the California boss told the New York mobster at the wedding. "For your man Molinas. You guys are cleaning up over there."

The New York mob guy shook his head in disbelief.

"That motherless fuck Jack Molinas? He is no friend of mine," he replied. "That piece of shit used my name?"

"Mysteriously," according to newspaper reports, the next morning, August 3, 1975, Jack Molinas was found shot in his driveway, right between the eyes. Coincidence? Maybe, but not likely. His girlfriend had also been shot in the head, but she lived. Molinas was doing all right at the time: He had three-quarters of a million dollars in the bank at the time he was killed.

"Stevie, that is exactly how I heard it, and there isn't anyone else still alive from back then who was there," my father said. "No one on the outside knows about it." Everyone knows now.

5

The Ends Justify the Means

STREET BOOKMAKING WAS a good living, but I always felt that I was meant to do much bigger things. I wanted more for myself than the street life had to offer—I wanted money in the bank, not cash under a mattress. I started thinking about going legit and starting at square one in the casino business with the grandiose plan of owning and operating my own casino one day. To do that, I had to learn how the big boys operated. I needed to learn how the entire legal gambling world worked— how big business was done, what to look for, what to avoid.

That meant one thing: Vegas, baby.

One of my dad's biggest clients when I worked for him in Miami was Aaron Genish, or "Mr. G.," as we called him. He was an Israeli businessman and real estate tycoon who was often called the Donald Trump of Israel. He would bet $100,000 a game, five games a night, seven days a week. A real whale. Mr. G. only knew about seven words of English, and his favorite one was "fan-taz-teak." When he called the office, he used to say, "Is me, Cowboys for $100,000, okay? Fan-taz-teak!"

It was a comedy show for the clerk writing his bet. Mr. G. was a huge casino player in Vegas and therefore had a ton of juice in that town, a town that he lost millions in on games like baccarat, craps, and roulette. Baccarat is a game played by high rollers in roped-off areas in casinos; Mr. G. could lose a million in a weekend at baccarat. He always seemed to earn more in his business than he lost at the tables, and in the end I heard he stiffed the town for close to $10 million in unpaid markers before he fled to Paris with the loot in tow. Before things went south for him, Mr. G. urged me to go to Las Vegas in the summer of 1992 to meet his connection at Caesar's Palace, a woman named Delores Owens, then the vice president of Caesar's World Marketing.

Something to keep in mind: Las Vegas is a town allegedly built by bookmakers. Charlie Meyerson, who ran the Golden Nugget and the Mirage and later the Bellagio, was reputed to be a former New York bookmaker. Some people even say that Steve Wynn's dad was a bookmaker, too, so the fact that I was a bookmaker wasn't likely to affect my standing, as long as I never got arrested. I mean, where else do you learn about gambling? In a college course? Back then, sports betting was a huge business for the casinos. But after the large publicly traded corporations took over Vegas, they have wanted nothing to do with sports betting. They see it as a liability compared to a slot machine, which does nothing but win a preprogrammed number of times. It takes too much work and human intervention to compete with the profit margins of slots and video poker, which combined are responsible for 80 percent of all casino revenue. That's right, it isn't blackjack or craps that makes the casino its money anymore—it's the slot machines! No longer is it the high roller at the craps table who moves the company's bottom line—it's his wife at the video poker machines playing for a dollar a hand.

The bottom line is that Vegas casinos have sportsbooks in them only because if they didn't, sports bettors would go to a hotel that did and play their blackjack, video poker, and slots while they were there.

In that initial meeting at Caesar's with Delores, we had a great talk. I was very open and told her gambling stories and what I knew about the business, and I could tell she appreciated my candor immensely. Most guys my age, twenty-two at the time, would have been severely intimidated by the VP of Caesar's Palace interviewing them and testing their overall gambling knowledge, but I was used to dealing with the highest level of gamblers and I had her eating out of the palm of my hand.

Looking to turn the vibe from that of a formal interview to a few buddies shooting the shit, I asked Delores if she wanted to hear about the first time I went to Vegas as an eighteen-year-old—an adult—without my parents.

"Sure," she said with a smile. We were very comfortable with each other already.

So I told her the story.

"I got to the room so excited to be in sin city alone and without parental guidance. I grabbed the yellow phone book from under the coffee table, went right to the 'escort service' page, and looked for the biggest hooker ad. And I dialed the phone number.

"'May I help you?' the voice that picked up purred.

"'Yes, this is Mr. Budin at the Mirage.' It was the first time I ever called myself Mr. Budin.

"'I'd like a Spanish girl, a black girl, and a white one. I want to watch the black and white ones go at it, and then we'll all join in.'"

Delores was looking at me like a deer in the headlights. I'm no idiot, I know that there comes a point in every story—a crossroad—where you're going to either totally tank or bring down the house. Needless to say, I usually brought down the house. Delores was looking at me like she had no idea where this was going. I mean, I was in an interview with the top dog at Caesar's World Marketing, not at a strip club with my buddies!

So I continued.

"The girl on the phone paused after I described, in detail, just what I wanted. Then she says, 'Mr. Budin, you have to dial a 9 to get an outside line here at the Mirage.'"

Delores broke out laughing, almost peed in her pants. She loved it. She called her secretary and had me retell the story. She was calling her friends, and we were leaving it on their answering machines.

And she wanted me to work for Caesar's immediately.

Delores was a straight shooter.

"As much as I'd like to get your twenty to twenty-five clients here," she said, "you are not quite ready to take over for me just yet. But what I can do is get you on board to run your own division of specialty marketing for us."

I was told I'd be operating junkets for Caesar's in both Vegas and Atlantic City. I brought all of my bookmaking clients on board, and we took off for weekends to Caesar's in both Vegas and Atlantic City. I ran the best junkets ever. I broke off a little from my father's business to focus on them, though I still ran my bookmaking business on the side. In fact, I was actually able to expand my bookmaking business by meeting new customers while in Vegas and Atlantic City, hosting trips for high rollers.

And these trips were incredible. I kept the clients plied with drugs and hookers, the best you could find on both counts.

Nothing was off-limits for my high rollers. Bets, drugs, and rock 'n' roll—it was a fantasy life for them, but it was my reality, my world, and I ran it like no one else ever had. They'd tell their friends about "the incredible weekend we had at Caesar's with Steve Budin," and I got more clients that way, both for the junkets and for my bookmaking business.

The job with Caesar's gave me the legitimacy I needed. It was an education in the legal betting world. I was the "executive junket rep" based out of Miami. I had my first business card. I started sending letters to my bookmaking clients. That was my first step toward running my own big-time legitimate betting business.

I had the best crew of stripper/hookers who worked for me on all my trips. No other rep was willing to go to the extremes I went to just to keep players happy while they lost their dough.

Word of mouth—"viral marketing"—helped me become the biggest and best in that division of the industry.

Once again, all the money I earned during that time went right out the window. The commission check I'd get from Caesar's would be gone as soon as I paid off the girls and took care of everything else I'd arranged for my clients. Here was the problem with the math: I'd get, say, $600 commission from a guy who lost $10,000, and that was nothing, because if that client lost the same amount on sports to my dad, I'd get 50 percent. My money from Caesar's was based on "theoretical win," and it just wasn't enough. I was bringing in guys who would bet hundreds of thousands of dollars—for what? Eighteen hundred dollars in commission plus free meals? Delores often doubled or tripled my commissions—I was making a rate better than guys who had been working for Caesar's for twenty years—but I wanted more.

After sucking every possible customer out of Caesar's and over to my bookmaking operation, which had swelled to its most voluminous state since I had taken it over, I started to figure that it was going to be tough to continue with Caesar's. I had to pay more attention to my bread and butter, and besides, I didn't feel that I was earning what I was worth. I couldn't just quit: The job provided me with a good cover, and I was addicted to being the big man in town. But the uneasiness I felt over the money I was making from Caesar's kept me looking for more ideas and different things to do.

Another bookmaking customer of ours from Florida was a guy named Sunny. A diplomat from Panama, he was also a private client of mine at Caesar's Palace.

Sunny was a member of the family that ruled Panama's government shortly after the U.S. took out Manuel Noriega. Sunny had been a big bettor for my father.

Sunny had gone on a couple of my junkets. We connected for a meeting one weekend in Atlantic City. Early one morning I got a call from Sunny after a night of gambling and boozing. At about 3:00 AM, he called my suite from the lobby and asked if he could come up. I said sure.

I always had a penthouse suite that I used to entertain my clients. I couldn't get all my players high-roller suites, as they didn't all merit them. That is why I always made sure I had a "phat pimp suite" for myself. I would use it as an open party suite for all my clients. I made sure everybody got the "complete" experience. I had a couple of girls with me at the time whose job it was to party in my room and flirt with my customers. I told them to get lost and give Sunny and me some privacy to talk.

I was pretty frustrated with the Caesar's gig at the time, because what I had thought would be an exciting, high-level gaming job was really nothing more than a glorified casino concierge gig. Guys would get pissed off that they didn't get breakfast for free and call me to complain. Here is a guy worth $5 million calling me to complain that he had to pay twenty-five bucks for breakfast? Wow. What the fuck do I say to that? On the one hand, the guy is right. He is a huge gambler and should get free eggs. On the other hand, who gives a flying fuck about twenty-five bucks when you're tipping cocktail waitresses "Benjamins" and betting $500 a hand?

Sunny was one of those complainers. He was the kind of guy who'd walk into the casino, order four bottles of Dom Perignon, empty out the minibar, take the pillowcases and towels, ask for tickets to any and all events, and get pissed when he got the bill. As I prepared for another round of typical bill negotiations, there was no way I could have foreseen the life-changing events that were about to take place.

Sunny came in and started talking, and I kept waiting for him to start beefing about this or that. He didn't. I learned when Sunny and I talked that day that his money came from his family being in power in Panama. His family, the Arangos, were one of only two ruling families that ever ran the government there, and when his family was in power, he would get concessions to run certain businesses in Panama. He made a ton of money that way, had multiple homes, and so on. He's a short guy who looks a lot like the actor Edward James Olmos, but he talks more like Cheech from Cheech and Chong.

Sunny looked at me dead in the eyes: "I have this . . . it's like a fucking license . . . to fucking gamble on sports in Panama," he said in broken English, with a strong accent. He also got a real kick out of cursing in English.

"What do you mean, you have a license?" I asked.

"I brung it with me," he said and pulled it out. "We make a fucking company to take fucking bets." Now he started to sound more like Tony Montana, but I was hanging in there and listening as closely as I could.

"A casino license?" I asked.

"No, no, the fucking casinos in Panama are run by the fucking government," he said. "This is a fucking bookie license. Sports bets."

He handed me the license. Bookmaking.

Holy shit.

This wasn't "like a fucking license." It *was* a license. An authentic government license. Sunny pulled out an English translation on fax paper of what the license was for. *Apuesta deportivas*—sports betting. He also had a contract in Spanish to prove its authenticity.

"Could you tell me about . . . how to do this?" he asked.

Sure I could. I knew everything about this kind of thing.

"Do you think this could be lucrative?" he asked.

Hell yes, I thought.

"If this is an exclusive license for sports betting, yes, it could be lucrative," I said.

"We make a deal with the fucking government," Sunny said. "They get a fucking cut, I get a fucking cut. I can write the fucking license to say whatever we want it to say."

Sunny had lost millions of dollars both betting with my dad over the years and gambling just as aggressively and recklessly at Caesar's.

I was thinking if we had three or four hundred guys like Sunny in Panama, we could easily have a business worth $10 million a year.

I sat there and talked with Sunny for six hours and drank a lot of champagne, all paid for by Caesar's, of course—you know Sunny. By the time I got done talking to him, I was ready to conquer Panama, wherever the fuck that was.

We cut the Panamanian government in as a 10 percent partner on gross profit—not including expenses, which could be 25 to 30 percent of the net. The exclusivity was the important thing: we'd be the only ones in all of Panama handling sports betting. There would be no competition.

"That's no fucking problem," Sunny said smiling. "You tell me. I write it. I get it fucking done."

Sunny was a blatant racist, as a lot of ruling-class Panamanians were. There were two types of Panamanians, light and dark, but no blacks. Sunny always called the "other" royal family "a bunch of niggers." He used to say, "They are as black as my phone," pointing to a system phone in his office. This was bizarre and very amusing to us because they were only slightly darker than him, and they certainly were not black. I truly despise racism, but the passion that Sunny would bring to his racist rants did prove hysterical over time—if only for its animated ignorance.

The other royal family was about to take power, Sunny explained, so time was of the essence. Sunny was splitting his share with his counterpart from the other family. This way, no matter who was in power, the license would always stand.

"We are going to bring in Ray Salas, whose father is a Supreme Court justice," Sunny said. "I know them twenty years; they will do whatever I say. They should kiss my ass for bringing you and your father to the table, fucking black-ass niggers!"

Sunny waxed poetical telling me about Panama. Unfortunately, my "bullshit detector" hadn't been fully developed yet and I bought into it completely, though the license itself was what I was after.

"Panama . . . it is like fucking paradise," he claimed orgasmically. "Overlook the waters of Balboa, and the ocean, all beautiful. You will fucking love it."

We hammered out a business plan and agreement.

Man, I thought to myself, *if there are even ten suckers like Sunny in the entire country, we have got it made.*

It was at that moment that I decided to leave everything behind and become a legit bookmaker for the people of Panama. I'd be the only bookmaker in the entire country! Hey, it wasn't Vegas, but it was a whole country. If nothing else, it was a move in the right direction, or so I thought.

6

Panama: Game On

WE FLEW TO Panama City in June 1994. There were three very busy streets, much like New York, so at first glance it looked like business would be great, because the people I saw on those streets looked like they had money. We only needed one hundred guys who bet like Sunny to have as big a business in Panama as my father and I had in the States.

But after those first three nice streets in Panama, the rest of the country was barren and impoverished. It was a Third World country. I didn't know it at the time, but Sunny had enlisted me in this venture because he was all tapped out. He had lost all his money gambling, and this was a last-ditch effort to get back on his feet and stay in the game. He had lost millions to Caesar's and millions to us. Totally bottomed out and nearly broke, he was looking for another con. I didn't know that coming into it, though. I thought his pockets were still lined deep. I would soon learn that Sunny was bringing me down there basically to rob me. I was too naive, but I was still building something myself and learning a lot about the industry, and doing business with Sunny would teach me an important lesson.

We set up our shop in Panama and went through all the licensing. The country opened my eyes to how others around the world live. Everywhere you looked there were soldiers, cops, or paramilitary guys in black clothes with silver stripes holding AK-47s. They wore dark glasses and motorcycle helmets and ran in posses. It was very disconcerting to go to the grocery store and see these guys—the government's police—in every aisle. They had all been soldiers in Noriega's army, and once he was removed from power, they went to work on the street as cops. That's not an easy transition to make, especially in a Third World country that, we quickly learned, was rife with corruption. These soldiers thought they were owed more from their country than a police job, and they extracted it in their own way.

I knew right away I wouldn't be able to "hire locally" for bodyguards: either they'd be in cahoots with Sunny or the government or they'd rob me blind. I did have some Colombian and Nicaraguan bodyguards, but I still brought down my own bodyguards from Miami—basically to protect me from my other locally hired bodyguards. I remember the moment I made that decision. One of my Nicaraguan guards said he liked the girls in Panama. He talked about how they were able to get girls back home—with guns!

"It's easy," he said. I remember thinking, *Where the hell am I?*

Needless to say, that comment prompted me to bring in my own people from Miami.

THE SUMMER OF 1994 was especially hot in Panama—more so than usual. And I don't mean just the temperature, which hovered around 96 degrees with 100 percent humidity; the country was transitioning from a dictator-led state under Noriega to a shaky democracy that felt more like old Russia than a U.S.-

styled democracy. After we took out Noriega, we just left the Panamanians to figure out a new government for themselves, because all we'd wanted was Noriega and the Panama Canal. Democracy did not take hold.

The entire country was run by a few last names, and depending on which ruling family was in charge, so went the good jobs, government contracts, and the reason we were there in the first place, the gambling license.

Arango was one of those last names, and Salas was another. One of our partners from the Panamanian government's side of the deal was Ray Salas. Sunny and Ray were both from a ruling family, but ones on opposite sides of the political aisle. Arango represented the rich, aristocratic political party, and Salas the blue-collar political party. With both an Arango and a Salas in on the deal, we were covered no matter which way the wind blew. It was a smart business model, at least when it came to government corruption in a Third World country.

I hit the job in Panama with unbridled enthusiasm and optimism. My hopes and ambitions shielded me from the ever-present reality that life in an oppressive, military-run country would never be acceptable to me in the long term—and of course I didn't realize that the same government model would keep my business from ever reaching its potential.

One of the first tasks was to hire employees. We ran a help-wanted ad in the paper that said, "International Sports Club Job in American sports related business—bilingual (English) and computer user."

Nine hundred people showed up to apply for what started out as ten jobs. We didn't need more than ten at first, though, because even if Sunny was right that there were "hundreds" of guys like him in Panama (I had my doubts after seeing the city),

I had written my own slips back in Florida with eight clerks for three hundred to four hundred clients. Even just twelve clerks would've been overkill.

But seeing those people shook us up. I looked at my friend Sandy Berger during one interview, to see if we were on the same page.

"Sandman, look at these people's faces. Do you see what I see?" I asked.

He did.

"This is going to be a very long day, my friend," he answered. "We are about to turn down nearly nine hundred applicants and send them home without the job they obviously desperately need to survive."

I looked at the crowd, and the scene was overwhelming. It was hot, and everyone was in his or her best suit, sweating like pigs in the un-air-conditioned lobby of the El Panama Hotel. We rented a conference room that Sunny hooked up for us. Who knows how much he made on that commission? At least $1,000 from the rooms, flights, and conference room rental—what a scumbag. We ended up deciding to hire fifteen clerks, and then twenty. Finally, we settled on twenty-five. We just had to give hope to as many people as we could.

I saw a lot of people that day, all with compelling stories, and all with a certain level of desperation in their eyes.

There were many standouts. Eduardo Herrera was one of them. His English was shaky and his computer skills limited, but he had a confidence and an inner light that was recognizable to all of us.

"Look, guys," he told Sandy and me. "You can look all over the world, but you will never find a more loyal soldier than me. Give me this opportunity, and you will never regret it."

It wasn't cocky, it wasn't rehearsed, and he just looked us in the eyes and meant every word he said. It was hard not to have a connection with him. He was a real man's man. I was not surprised after reading his résumé to learn that he'd been a lieutenant in Noriega's army and was now a "deactivated" soldier, even though he'd earned many medals of honor. He was loyal and honorable. It turns out that he was a trained assassin, too. Ironically, he was also a sweetheart of a guy who would eventually become like a brother to me.

WE STILL HAD the rest of the business to set up. We had about two months to figure out what we were doing, and there was a fight every step of the way, from Sunny wanting a piece of every dollar we spent to everyone else we dealt with wanting money on the side—a licensing fee, if you will. Sunny wanted to "help." He found us a little garage that he said we could lease for $10,000 a month—of which he'd get five grand, I learned. I contacted a real estate broker. Before I even met with the guy, Sunny found out I had called him and went to the broker— that's how small a place this was. It was like a fixed blackjack game we couldn't get out of.

We fought through it the best we could. We let Sunny rob us a little, but not a lot. We were getting charged for all these "fees" he had never mentioned, ones that I had never heard of anywhere. An "education fee," an "import tax" of $1,500 for $20,000 worth of machinery we had ordered. Sunny just kept inventing taxes.

We didn't want a garage for our business. We needed a building that was upscale and exuded the corporate image we were building. Sandy and I were dressed every day in spectacular suits and silk ties—it actually became a daily best-dressed competition between us. That was part of our business philosophy: You don't look the part of a *Fortune* 500 CEO if you're wearing a trench coat with betting slips and parlay cards dangling from your pockets.

The nicest and newest building in Panama was the new AT&T building on the Balboa River. Overlooking a river sounds nice, right? Actually, it looked more like a sewage dump. But the building was gorgeous. We signed a lease for $4,000 a month, which even without paying a "commission" to Sonny was an extortionary rate. But we had to have a nice place to do business if we were going to attract the local betting crowd, especially the high-end clientele that Sunny promised me existed. Remember, our entire focus at this point was to exclusively book the local Panamanian bets.

WE FINALLY GOT the business opened. With no Internet (and I doubt there is to this day for the common folks in Panama), we did all of our bet-taking by phone. The locals had to come in and make a deposit, and then they could bet. Since our office was in a bank building, I thought that once we opened we'd have four hundred customers doing $10 parlays and placing all kinds of bets. But it was quiet as could be. Not a single person came in the whole day.

Toward the end of that first day, Mr. Towatchi, a local businessman, came in and was really pumped up. He was well dressed but was looking for credit. I double-checked that Towatchi had big businesses and extended him $100,000 in credit, something I'd never have done back in the States. Naturally, he lost $100,000 the first week. I realized that I had gotten myself into a collection situation in a country that was unfriendly to Americans. I didn't have the same strengths and help that I had in the United States. I couldn't say, "Pay me my money, or else!" He had given me a $100,000 check to hold. But he admitted that he couldn't cover it. In Panama he would have faced serious repercussions for writing such a huge bad check. So I worked out a deal with him for $50,000: he had to sell his car, empty his bank accounts, and get a loan against his home.

Two weeks later, we still had no local business. There were only perhaps 1,500 people in the entire country who could afford to eat out in restaurants. Panama was poverty-stricken. Of course, Sunny had never told me any of this. He was robbing me from the time I set foot in Panama because he knew a sports betting business couldn't work there—and that he couldn't deliver any of what he'd promised.

I had been making big money in my bookmaking business in the States, and I gave it up for this: nothing. I had the idea that being a bookie for a country where sports gambling is legal was the way to go. I still believed that, but I knew it wasn't going to happen in Panama with Panamanian clients.

In a word, Panama was hell. There was a separation of class in that country between rich and poor that I had never seen in my life. There was a small group of very rich people, and everyone else was poor. This oppression was breathed in like air. The poor were willing to accept the oppression, and the wealthy were glad to force it down their throats. The poor had no aspirations to ever being upper-class, partly because the upper class ruled with an iron fist. It was a dirty life. The poor were all darker-skinned and the rich all lighter-skinned. It was sickening. There were no outside newspapers in Panama. The idea was to keep everybody dumb. Dumb and drunk. That was the only way to keep the poor from wising (and rising) up.

• • •

BETS, DRUGS, AND ROCK & ROLL

SINCE THE BUSINESS showed no signs of life despite my best efforts, I turned to an old gambling client of my dad's, the legendary television sports gambling evangelist Stu Feiner. Feiner, the top telephone handicapper in the United States, came to the rescue for me. I called him up to check an old gambling figure and to make arrangements to settle. Stu was touting hundreds of clients while also supplying thousands of gamblers with scores and odds via his nationally recognized "Scorephone." Remember, before the Internet you couldn't just click and find out scores; you had to call your local newspaper and ask a reporter to check the Associated Press wire, or you had to call someone like Stu Feiner and his score phone. Bettors calling his Scorephone would hear the scores and odds and then Stu himself, in his "Crazy Eddie"–style banter, selling his daily best bet. He had a huge following and was really the first handicapper to tap phone-in customers as a source of revenue for his handicapping business.

"Stu, I'm dying out here," I said. "I left a great job at Caesar's, and of course my own bookmaking business, and there isn't shit here. Stu, look, I don't know what I'm doing. I'm thinking about throwing in the towel. And by the way, you still owe the old man $24,000. How do you want to handle it?"

Stu paused. He didn't want to see me give up, and more importantly, he didn't want to pay me. Stu was a salesman, not quite a con man, but clearly the best in his business. Stu was a lot like crime, and you know what they say about crime—it never pays! Stu hated to pay. Don't get me wrong, Stu always paid his debts in the end, and never fucked anyone over for money. It was just the collecting from Stu was like pulling teeth. He started scheming and talking his way around an idea that would get him out of paying his debt.

"Listen," he said. "I have this free 'Scorephone' that bettors call to get scores from their games. How about we put some ads for your company on my phones and into my schedules that I mail out and we forget the money I owe you?"

"You think people are going to call us from the States when they can bet with their local bookmaker?" I asked.

"You're right. It would never work," he said.

That night, however, I replayed the conversation in my mind. There was a nugget to be gleaned from our talk. What if U.S. bettors started playing with us? From my initial conversation with Sunny up until I talked to Stu that night, I had never considered U.S. bettors as potential clients.

Why not? I asked myself. I sat upright in bed as the realization hit me. I was about to change the entire way the bookmaking world worked. Panama was not, and never would be, a gambling mecca. But I could change the bookmaking world, and make a mint from Panama, if I had U.S. bettors.

Game on.

7

The Dream

DIDN'T SLEEP THE rest of the night. How could I? The whole plan unfurled in front of me. I started thinking of all the advantages I could offer my clients from an offshore location. One of the biggest problems for bettors in the United States was that when it came time to pay, it wasn't as easy as putting it on your credit card. You had to come up with cold hard cash, and if you couldn't, you were liable to catch a beating. Then there was the law to contend with. What if the corner bookie got caught? Try to get paid when your bookie gets busted.

This was it. The plan was hatched.

We would set up a system with computers. We'd take the bets over the phone and enter them into a central computer system that would manage the money, take the bets, and process the credit cards. I didn't know a lot about how computer systems worked at the time, but I knew that I could find someone who did.

Here was the dream. We would offer U.S. residents a professional, businesslike telephone bookmaking service, fully equipped with customer service, credit card processing, and twenty-four-hour access to call and wager. This would be the polar opposite of what was currently available to bettors with their local bookie. This would be like switching from Nathan's to Morton's.

So I went to work. The credit cards would be great, because we could get authorization codes and keep them on file. And what would happen when bettors maxed out their credit cards? They would go out to the mailbox the next day and there would be another credit card offer. And another. The credit card bettor still had an easy out at that time—bankruptcy. The way the credit card industry was set up then—and still is to a large extent—was as a nonthreatening line of credit that almost invited you not to pay in the end. They advanced you more than you could afford so that they could assess that monthly fee and be in your pockets for years to come and collect far more than you ever charged. That's how the goodfellas did it: they'd advance more than their customers could pay so that they could shylock them the rest of their lives on points. The credit card companies are no less ruthless. The longer I've been in business, the more I've found out about the parallels between the corporate world and the mob and the way they conduct business—especially the credit card companies.

I got Sunny in the office the next day and told him I needed a new license. I told him we weren't making any money and wouldn't make any money unless I could get a new license, one that would allow me to take bets from the United States.

Sunny hit us up for another one of his BS "government" fees. Bo and Donnie, my silent New York partners, were already into the deal for millions, and I had to ask for more. So I pitched them on my plan. I didn't want hundreds of bettors—I wanted thousands, and phones ringing all day. They bought into it hook, line, and sinker.

There were bookmakers on every corner in New York and Miami, but they were shady characters, and bettors were scared of many of them. The rest of the bookmakers were pretty much con artists. Bettors worried that all bookmakers were tied to the mob. My business would present them with a corporate betting atmosphere that would make them feel safe. And what about all the bettors in rural and middle America? Who were they betting with? There are no real bookmakers in Montana. There are no bookmakers in Tennessee.

Another big problem for bettors was collecting, but that wouldn't be the case with my business. We'd pay off our "winners" twenty-four hours a day, seven days a week. That was unheard of, because the bookmaker usually had to collect before he could pay out, which meant tracking down guys for the money they had lost the weekend before. If you won on a weekend, you were lucky to get paid by Thursday. More often, it could take weeks if the bookmaker was overextended. Offshore, with proper banking in place and using FedEx and Western Union, we'd pay everyone who won on a seven-day-a-week basis, no exceptions and no excuses. That would give people the confidence to post their money up, albeit via credit card, with an international bookmaker.

We were headed for the sports gambling world's promised land, and I could feel it.

I hired the best lawyers in the United States, and they got manuals for Sandy and me on money laundering—how to avoid it, what was and wasn't considered laundering, and so on. I didn't want to run afoul of the law. We had to pay U.S. taxes—that was essential. And we would always do that.

If bettors wanted to play $20,000 per game, no problem—we'd pay them right away if they won. I picked up about twenty-five guys right away who had bet with me in the past, in the streets, and converted them to offshore players.

I called Stu Feiner back and offered him a deal: a fifty-fifty split on our profit. Stu turned it down. He needed cash up front because he was always overextended with loans from shady shylocks, and he always owed bookmakers tons of money, too. Stu Feiner was portrayed by Al Pacino in *Two for the Money,* a film about the life of star handicapper Brandon Lang. Like his character in the movie, Stu always needed cash and would sell off tomorrow and the next day to get it today. Had he taken my offer of a fifty-fifty split, he'd have cleared a million bucks within a year, and as a partner he'd have had exponentially more than that on the way. Not Stu. He wanted his $350,000 right then and there.

"Send me $350,000, and I'll give you a whole year," he said.

"Done," I answered. This was a steal. And I'm not an idiot: I didn't send him the whole $350,000 in advance. I sent him $50,000 at a time. We had five phone lines the day the ads started running on Stu's Scorephone, which provided free scores in every city. The phone lines lit up in our office and never stopped ringing. There were so many calls coming in that the phone lines literally broke—they went out. I was told that we received more calls that day than the entire rest of Panama had in the same time period.

That was the beginning of the technology issues that would ultimately force us to consider leaving Panama (and, oh yeah, the fact that everyone we dealt with was crooked), but the good news was that we also knew we had something big on our hands, something huge. Sunny came back and wanted $5,000 a month additional for the new betting license. This would supposedly go to the city's mayor—who was, ironically, his second cousin. To be honest, we'd have paid Sunny $20,000 a month—we were glad he was such a petty thief.

We grew to eight phone lines after six weeks. That was a big change from the first six weeks, when we received just one phone call—asking us to move a car we had parked illegally out in front of the building!

We were getting seventy to eighty phone calls every half-hour, more than five hundred calls per day. Sunny hit us up again for $400 for "cab fees" and other expenses—he was just making stuff up. But it was small compared to the money we were already raking in.

I was twenty-five years old and had tens of thousands of dollars coming in, and hundreds of thousands the next month. Things were certainly getting interesting.

ONE OF THE things we had to do when we got on our feet in Panama was to find cars for ourselves. Using taxis was a pain, and using drivers who were loyal to Sunny gave us no privacy—he'd know when we left, where we went, what we talked about, what we bought, and even what we shopped for. So Sandy Berger and I walked down to a used-car lot just two blocks from our office. Sunny had hoped to hook us up with cars, but we knew his cut or finder's fee—or ridiculous made-up tax—would drive the cost far higher than the market average.

We got to the lot, and I was pretty set on getting a Land Rover or similar SUV.

The salesman, though, had other ideas. Alberto Moke showed us this old Mercedes-Benz sedan. This thing, in its day, might have been some kind of vehicle, but at this point it was a piece of shit. It had curtains in the back, was a much older model than I wanted, and even by Panamanian standards wasn't a "nice ride."

But this kid Moke was shaking and baking—a real sales tiger. He could sell a drowning man a glass of water, and I was guzzling as he spewed his pitch. Sandy and I were convinced we needed this car.

We wrote him a check and headed to the car. Sandy and I looked at each other.

"What just happened?" I asked.

"I'm not quite sure," Sandy said. "He said it's a good car, though."

"Yeah, yeah, he said that," I answered. "Well, if it's half as good as he made it sound. . . ."

It didn't make it halfway back to the office—which was only two blocks away! The air conditioning—a key point in his sell to us—didn't work. We got one block off the lot, and the lemon broke down. It wouldn't start, wouldn't even turn over—it just broke down in the middle of the road.

Sandy and I looked at each other and broke down laughing.

"Holy shit," I said. "We were bluffed. He got us."

"He sure did," Sandy said. "Helluva salesman."

We left the car in the street and walked back to his office.

"You're taking this piece of shit car, and giving us back our money," I said.

"No, no, it's a great car," Moke said. "And if there's a problem, I've got another one that has your name all over it. I even thought when you guys drove away—I have this 1976 Audi with air conditioning that would make you think you're at the North Pole." The kid was already back in full hard-sell mode. It was amazing. We let him talk for a second, and then I cut him off.

"No, you don't understand. You *are* taking this car back," I said.

He looked at me, very disappointed. He started to launch into another sales pitch.

"No, listen," I said. "How much do you make here?"

He appeared disappointed.

"Four hundred dollars a month," he answered.

"Take this car back, give me my check back, and you're going to come work for me," I said. "And I'm going to pay you six hundred fifty a month to help me run my company."

"After this, you want to hire me?" he asked.

"Hell, yes," I said. "If you can fool me and Sandy here, I need you on my team. I own the new sportsbook in the AT&T building, and I need someone who can help me convince people in America to send money to Panama to bet."

"I could do that," Alberto said.

"I need someone who understands the Panamanian culture, who can sift through the bullshit these guys sell me when I need my phones fixed, when I need stuff for my office, or when I need anything," I said.

"I can do that," Alberto said confidently.

Alberto joined our staff, and while neither he nor anyone else could make all the hassles of Panama go away, he did a nice job. We grew to trust him. He was a fun guy to have around the office. His father, oddly enough, was a preacher.

Alberto was also in charge of arranging hookers for our VIPs, executive staff, and guests. He did a great job. We would call him, and he would get a lineup of local girls to meet us at the Burger King closest to the office. The girls, ranging in age from eighteen to twenty-two, would line up against the Burger King wall, and we would basically start ordering take-out. At $50 a girl, we'd always wind up taking almost all of them.

· · ·

BETS, DRUGS, AND ROCK & ROLL

WHEN WE FIRST started taking bets locally, former Noriega Army officer and interview-day standout Eduardo Herrera didn't have the English-speaking skills to be on the A shift of clerks, so we put him on the B shift. The A shift worked on game days— Saturday, Sunday, and Monday. The B shift worked off days— Tuesday, Wednesday, Thursday, and Friday—when there was less traffic and we could better assess their skills and potential. The idea was to give the less talented workers a chance to grow on nonhectic days before we threw them into the fire on a game day.

I immediately noticed Eduardo's talent. Not so much in working the phones, but as a leader in the room. Everyone looked up to him and admired him. His talent quickly caught up to his ambition, and he became the lead clerk on the first phone of the B shift. He was not only answering 75 percent of the incoming calls but doing all the line inputting into the main computer. That last part was supposed to be the job of Howie, a guy New York sent us to be our head bookmaker; it turned out that Howie was not only incompetent but a spy for our backers.

Howie, like everyone, loved Eduardo and moved him to the A shift, mostly because of his ability to enter the lines and keep the staff in order. By that point, I realized there was no need for Howie. My dad was making and setting the lines from home in Florida and dictating them to Howie, who had Eduardo entering them and handling the staff. My dad was constantly on the phone with Howie checking the tallies and moving the lines, only to have Eduardo actually make the moves.

However, I noticed that while Howie was on the phone a lot, it wasn't with my dad. I had the phone guy in Panama, Andaluz, set me up a way to eavesdrop on Howie's calls. He was calling back to Bo and Donnie in New York every minute, telling them every little bullshit detail, from who was fucking hookers to which secretaries were flirting with me to who was hanging out under my desk. He was a rat shill put there by New York to protect their interests and egos. So I decided Howie had to go. It was a delicate situation because he was Bo and Donnie's spy, but the truth was that he was just getting in the way and we were all confident that Eduardo could run the show and take direction on the lines and odds from my dad directly, without Howie running interference.

In the coming weeks, my dad came to Panama to visit. He loved to come to Panama. I made sure all my secretaries paid special attention to him whenever he came into town, if you know what I mean. We were holed up in the conference room discussing the pressing need to get Howie out. Earlier, my dad had asked Howie for a score on the Nebraska game, as we had a big decision pending on it. About an hour went by while we ate lunch. Suddenly Howie barged in without knocking. I looked at him and said, "Hey, what the fuck, you don't knock?"

He looked like he swallowed his tongue and just stood there.

"So what the fuck is it? What is so important?" my dad asked him.

Howie said nothing.

I stood up.

"Howie, I'm gonna ask you one more time," I said. "What the fuck is it that is so important that you barged in here and interrupted our lunch?"

He looked at my dad and said, "I just wanted to give you an update on that Nebraska game, Dave."

My dad sat back down, figuring Howie had both good news and good intentions.

"So, Howie," Dad said. "What's the update?"

"We lost it in the last second," Howie answered.

There is an unwritten rule in bookmaking that goes back to the streets, where I was trained: You never give bad news to a boss unless specifically asked.

In fact, if you are even asked if you know, you are better off saying you don't know and waiting for the instruction to go look it up. You never offer a bad score unless you are specifically asked to retrieve it and report it. As our head bookmaker, Howie should have known about this very serious ethical code. He had broken *another* cardinal rule.

To make matters worse, no one is more old school than my father, a born and bred Brooklyn hustler. Howie had just insulted my father's manhood and professional standing in the business.

My dad rose to his feet sensing the opportunity to use this incident to do away with that rat Howie once and for all.

"I will tear your fucking eyes out of your fucking head, you cocksucker," he yelled. I jumped in front of my dad, as he was ready to make good on that promise.

"Hold on, Dad," I said, putting both hands on his chest. My dad stood six-foot-four, 265 pounds of solid mainframe, and even at sixty-four years old, he could scare the shit out of a mountain lion.

I turned to Howie.

"You'd better fucking turn around and go, fast, and never come back," I said. "You are finished. Pack your shit and get the fuck out of here."

Howie took my advice and ran out. By that time the entire office had heard my dad's roar and gathered outside the conference room doors. Howie came out white as a ghost and never looked at anyone—just walked out the front door and never returned.

This was genius on my dad's part. Bo and Donnie were old school. They couldn't say shit, since they would have done the exact same thing. They couldn't send a new guy, either, because we had told them we were ready to promote Eduardo, who we already knew was better than Howie. Besides, we trusted Eduardo. Bo and Donnie would literally have to ask to put in another spy, and they weren't ready to do that. It was the perfect crime, and it got that rat Howie out of our office for good.

What we couldn't have yet known was that Eduardo would not only meet but exceed our expectations. He picked up the ball and ran with it—the exact opposite of Howie. Eduardo was a details guy who was always willing to take direction and criticism from both my dad and myself. He became a top bookmaker in the industry and would go on to run many other sports gambling businesses in the future. This was all thanks to the training he received under my dad's direction. He remained honest, loyal, and extremely productive till the last day of the business.

SANDY WAS A godsend to have along for the ride. Aside from his considerable legal expertise, he spoke Spanish fluently. I'd end up picking it up in a few months myself, but I never could speak it like a native. Sharp dressed and articulate, smart and bilingual, Sandy was a big key to this thing working.

Sandy helped do the talking to help solve our phone problems. Nico Barletta, the son of the former Panamanian president, ran the government-controlled phone company at the time. Just weeks into the new setup, I knew eight phone lines wouldn't be enough. We needed twenty-five phone lines, and

counterbalanced all of the negativity for a while, it ultimately started me on the road to excess and self-destruction. While I didn't go out like Tony Montana, it got pretty damn close there for a while.

Next door to our office building was a little place called Passion Fruit, where I used to entertain my managers and top employees all the time. It was basically a massage parlor/whorehouse with very young women who looked like models and would do anything for $35. I remember treating my supervisors for lunch every Friday there. I called it "having the surf-and-turf special." Then I would come back to the office and go upstairs on the roof and smoke three of the fattest joints I could roll.

I had started having my driver Luis fly back and forth to Miami to smuggle in the good weed, because the Panama weed was the absolute worst crap I had ever seen. Being in Panama was very tough and tested my every resource, but being there straight was just impossible. I'd come down from the roof and fuck this little maid in the broom closet in the office. She was so hot, spoke no English, and we never said a word to each other. I loved my wife; my wife was gorgeous, smart, and a loving mother, too. I mean, let's face it, I was never going to leave my wife for a Panamanian maid, but Panama was a man's country, and it was tough to resist the daily temptations available in excess there.

Don't get me wrong—just thinking about Panama literally hurts my head to this day. We were constantly fighting the infrastructure problems and corruption. The problems reached their zenith when the phone system went down for, no kidding, probably the hundredth time. This time was a big crash, though. The Telemuxes that Brian Green had gotten us were crap—this crash told us that definitively. We threw all the Telemuxes in the trash.

This should have been an exciting time because we were taking international calls, and I had gone from a handful of clerks to twenty-five—an operation five times bigger than I had ever seen or than I had ever run myself. So the phones going down now was costing us thousands of dollars an hour—and probably much more considering that some bettors, needing their gambling "fix," would simply seek out another bookmaker. This was bad, bad business. We had a great idea, but were failing miserably on the execution.

The phones had crashed, though, because our new operation with twenty-five clerks was extremely successful. The phone lines literally burned up from overuse, and there were problems with the hundreds who were trying to call while our clerks were tied up taking bets.

This was a Friday night, and we couldn't make it through the weekend without phones. Not in the middle of football season, which was when we took the most action.

I stayed in the office around the clock trying to help fix the problem, which went on for several days. I had to pull our advertising to stop calls from coming in. Of course, no money was coming in, either.

Roberto Ross, the tech guy from the Panama phone company, was our local representative. He was doing the best he could, but he was also doing something he'd never done before, on a scale he'd probably never imagined, so he was working in the dark. He didn't know that Brian Green had sold us trash for equipment and that the Telemuxes couldn't be fixed because they were outdated or simply could not do what we were told they were designed to do.

But there Roberto and I were, in the office, night after night. He had a charming accent, very strong, so much so that it was hard to understand him when he tried to speak in his broken English.

As is usually the case when something breaks down, nobody took responsibility. The carrier people blamed Panama, and the Panamanians blamed the carrier company. The phone company claimed it wasn't their problem, yet we had no phone service. No one had an answer—it was just finger-pointing.

This went on for two god-awful weeks. No revenue, but expenses out the ass as everyone nickel-and-dimed me only to ultimately say they couldn't help me or that the problems weren't theirs.

Finally, after Sprint told us it wasn't their problem—they had tested their international phones with three other local companies and those worked just fine—Roberto came out looking happy.

"Da hamster!" Roberto said. "The problem is wit da hamster!"

Delirious from not sleeping and whacked out on weed, I was trying to imagine a hamster on a wheel somewhere that had finally passed out or had a little hamster heart attack and keeled over.

"Hamster?" I asked.

He shook his head yes again and again.

This went on for almost fifteen minutes.

"This has to do with a rodent somewhere?" I asked another guy. The fellow cast a puzzled look.

"Hamster," he said. "Your phone base—Hamster, Floreeda—that's where the problem is."

Homestead, Florida! It dawned on me finally. All of our traffic ran through the phone office in Homestead, run by Josh, infamous telephone tech to all international bookies. We had overlooked the Homestead office because that hadn't been the problem before, so we had no reason to think it was this time either.

I called my father.

"The problem is in Homestead—with our phones," I said.

"I'll get dressed and bang on their door within the hour," he said. "I'll grab that fuck Josh by the throat myself and shake him into compliance."

The problem, we found out from Josh in Homestead, was that we had to plug in a new router.

That was it.

So after all of my twelve-hour shifts and twenty-two-hour days in the office, we plugged one thing into the wall, and the phones started ringing off the hook. We summoned all the clerks and went back to work.

While it was great to be back in business—I called and started the ads running again, and we were already at maximum capacity within sixty minutes of the phones working again—the frustration of having something so small take days to solve and being bilked by locals for "fixes" or off-base "diagnosis" made me realize that Panama was a dead end for us.

We had reached our capacity with twenty-five clerks. We were making great money at that point, no question about it. But the constant fires we had to put out were not only burning me out but burning precious dollars by the tens of thousands on a weekly, sometimes even daily, basis.

As I looked out at all the phones ringing, saw all my clerks taking bets, and checked the thousands pouring into our account in that first hour, I shook my head: We were just scratching the surface here. I could take in more than a few million a year here with twenty-five clerks, but what if I were in a place that had the technology to handle one hundred clerks, or even two hundred clerks? What if I didn't have to deal with local corruption and a government that had its hand out every single day?

Throughout the whole crisis of the router problem, Brian Green, still left over from Rodrigo the Cuban, was of surprisingly little help and acted weirder than usual—which is saying something for an open cocaine-addicted polygamist.

So while the router issue had passed, we still had some dirt to sweep out the door. Rodrigo had sold us on Brian as a "computer genius." In reality, Brian was an opportunist who hired a Costa Rican programmer named William Ramirez to do all of his work for him. Panama in itself was just one big problem. Another day meant another half-dozen fires to put out. Brian turned out to be one of the bigger fires, and he tried his best to burn us for everything he could, starting with those seven-year-old Telemuxes that were worth zero.

Brian was an American who was deep into cocaine and had several wives. My own view was, "Your shit is your shit, but don't drag it into the office. Just do your job." Unfortunately, the number of other qualified candidates to run computers where we were in Panama was zero—especially for what we needed done.

Still, we knew Brian was not only ripping us off but thinking of even more ways to steal from us. We weren't sure how, but we just knew it. We didn't need this guy working on our computers, since those were our lifeline to the business and also had a lot of sensitive information on them—money, credit card numbers, and so on. The one good thing that came out of Brian via Rodrigo the Cuban, however, was the opportunity to bring William Ramirez on board from Costa Rica to help with the computers.

As I said, I knew Brian was plotting something, and I was certain he was already ripping us off. While I didn't know much about computers, I knew a lot about people. And I knew Brian was a bad seed. So one day I called in the security guy we called El Churrio. He was from—and named after—the worst and toughest neighborhood in Panama, just over the bridge from our office. We were located on one of the only two nice streets in the country, but just over the bridge it was like Spanish Harlem, with hoodlums everywhere. El Churrio was about six-foot-ten and easily four hundred pounds. I pointed toward Brian, and then the door. "Get Brian out!" I ordered.

My father and I took William for a ride that day. William recalls it as "the day your father and you kidnapped me. I thought you were going to put concrete shoes on me and toss me in the Panama Canal." My father and I grabbed William to get him out of the office before Brian could reach him and brainwash him. So we threw him into the car and drove away. Brian would tell William anything—that we were criminals, that we were the ones trying to rob him, kill him, just anything.

We were acting like we were very upset. I knew William wasn't into money. He's a thinker, an intellectual. And he happens to be very honest.

Besides being a big man, my dad looks kind of like Tony Soprano—very intimidating, especially if you don't know him. If he's screwed with, he can back it up—he's an old-school bookmaker who can, just by talking to you, make you shit your pants. We were ready to bring William on board to replace Brian, and we wanted him to respect us and fear consequences for anything out of order.

We took William out of the car by the water.

"Do have a problem with us, William? You have one chance

to tell us," my dad said calmly, but with enough implied force to knock down a tree. "Tell us everything. You have one shot. Tell us everything now, and you do right by us, and we go into the future together."

William was literally shaking. He was in full panic mode—fight or flight, though neither was an option. We were standing out on a pier, and it certainly must have seemed like we were going to kill him. I can't say that impression wasn't by design.

"I had nothing to do with it!" William pleaded. "Brian was designing a software program to siphon off your money—a hole in the program to produce fake winners. But I never had anything to do with it. Stevo . . . you know I'd never do anything like that to you! I'm sorry."

We were shocked beyond belief. We had no idea we were going to hear this. When William spilled it, something happened; we created an even deeper bond. William could have split after that, but he wasn't going to. He liked us and enjoyed working with us. As a thinker, he liked working on the challenges we faced. He had just been caught in the middle with Brian. So this freed not just us but William also, since he was able to quit working for that freak.

Again, we had no idea of Brian's plot and were not trying to scare William into a confession. It just happened that way. We ended up having a great talk with William after he told us about Brian's foiled plan. William started talking about Costa Rica as we looked around at the abject poverty and environmental degradation that was the city of Panama—the place was a shithole.

"I studied in college. . . . I've been a computer scientist and a college professor, and my father is a scientist. You would not even be able to comprehend the stark contrast of Costa Rica," William said. "Panama is not representative of what life is like throughout Central America. In Costa Rica it's a pure democracy. Education is important. So is the environment."

I listened to William, and he was selling me his dream, just like I sold him and everyone else working for me the dream I had for the business. We had spent a lot of time smoking pot and building the program together the last few weeks, and we both found common ground bitching about Panama. In fact, the day William was hired he had stumbled upon a riot coming to our office. He had been teargassed right in the face and came into our office completely shaken up; the expression on his face seemed to say: "What in the hell have I gotten myself into?" He hated Panama as much as the rest of us. But more than that, he was offended by the conditions, the fraud, the lack of care for the environment, and the class separation.

"You think I'm a good programmer? There are hundreds like me in Costa Rica," William pleaded passionately. "People here in Panama are still playing Atari— that's a computer to them! We need to get the hell out of this place, Stevo!"

I couldn't have agreed more.

8

The Sky's the Limit: Costa Rica

PANAMA WAS A disaster. We were tired of the daily battles, the corruption, and the dozens of other problems that the country confronted us with. My marriage was suffering. Even though my wife was a trouper, living in Panama was dangerous. She was pregnant by then, and Panama was no place for an American woman to have and raise a child. I moved her back to Miami until I could figure out where to move the business. We were too big for Panama. They did not have—and probably still don't have—the technological infrastructure for our business. And our profits would always be choked off by the rampant fraud and corruption. I had looked at Antigua and a few other places. But William's description of Costa Rica intrigued me. It was incongruent with my Panamanian-based impression of Central America, but if Costa Rica was half of what William said it was, it would be exponentially better than Panama.

After nine months in Panama, we made plans, as clandestinely as we could, to go visit Costa Rica for a little research and development. We told our Panamanian partners that it was a trip to acquire a new credit card processor. Sandy, William, and I got on a plane and had already left Panama behind before we left the ground.

As the American Airlines plane descended into Costa Rica, we were breathless. All we could see were green mountains and endless beauty. I've never been to Switzerland, but this is what I envisioned it would look like, without the snow.

Once we landed and got off the plane, I could see stark differences from Panama. No armed cops in black riot gear in helmets—in fact, the Costa Rican police didn't even carry guns. People were moving about and talking pleasantly, whereas in Panama it was all shouting and confrontation, with people scurrying about. Even the diction was different. In Panama it was harsh and rash, whereas Costa Rican speech was more Argentina aristocratic. Costa Rica was, as William said, a different land, a different people, and a whole different way of life from Panama.

Costa Rica had a true democracy more than one hundred years old, with an elected president, whereas ruthless dictators had ruled Panama for a very long time. While education was limited in Panama, Costa Rica provided free education for all of its citizens from kindergarten through college. Even our cab driver had a college degree and was very well spoken and pleasant.

Our plan was to shut down the business in Panama, move it, and bring over our existing customers in a smooth transition to Costa Rica. We all fell in love with the country right away; it was like a utopia compared to Panama. I called my wife and sold her on the dream, told her how beautiful Costa Rica was, and made plans to bring her down. I was always selling the dream, to the investors, to the employees, to the customers, and to myself. Now I was selling the dream to my wife, and she was always a tough sell, no matter what I was negotiating for.

Everyone we dealt with in Costa Rica was educated and articulate. And right there by the airport was the SARET free trade zone in the city of Allajuela, a perfect spot for a business.

Our first stop was at the lawyers' offices. We sat with some of the most prominent lawyers in Costa Rica, including Jorge de la Guardia and José Juan Sabrado. Jorge had been an adviser to the president of Costa Rica. Obviously, we hired him for his political influence, though he was also a top-notch attorney.

We had to find out if what we planned to do was legal. It took us about an hour to explain to José and Jorge what our business was about and how it would operate. There were bookmakers in Costa Rica at the time, but not at the highly visible commercial level. Most of them were people like Monte and Ron Sacco, who had at one time run illegal businesses in the United States and had moved them offshore to avoid prosecution. Sacco and his ilk moved offshore to fly under the radar, whereas we were on billboards and advertised very much in the open in America. We were also in a gray area, however, because while bookmaking was illegal in the U.S., we weren't in the U.S.

"There is no law in the Costa Rican constitution that bans, or approves, what you do," Jorge told us. He added with a smile, "There is also no law that approves waking up in the morning, but people who do that aren't arrested."

We did present ourselves publicly, though not as a bookmaking operation but as a telemarketing business that sold sports magazine subscriptions, just to stay as low as we could until the business got up and going. Everyone in the know, however, knew what we were doing.

We laughed and smiled. Jorge understood us. We were told that the Costa Rican constitution was over a hundred years old and hadn't been changed save for one amendment in fifty years. One point we kept pushing was that we'd add over two hundred well-paying jobs. The main industries were still bananas and coffee, so the educated workforce had few options. Technological jobs were few and far between. We talked about starting out with no fewer than one hundred phone lines and two hundred "booths" where the clerks would take phone calls and process bets. Two hundred jobs got their attention.

"Of course you can do it," Jorge said after making a few phone calls. We had a written opinion from Jorge and José—it wasn't a license—that said it was legal. It wasn't a sure thing, but it sure beat waiting for the phones to break again in Panama or sitting in a basement in Brooklyn waiting for the cops to break down the door.

WILLIAM'S BEST FRIEND in Costa Rica was Percy Gonzalez, the head of international phone business for ICE, which was the telephone company in Costa Rica.

I can never forget when I first met Percy. We were having telephone problems in Panama, and I asked William if he knew anyone in Costa Rica who was the telephone equivalent of what he was in the computer department. By this time I had completely given up hope that we would ever find a competent Panamanian technical service provider.

William knew Percy from the tech scene in Costa Rica and invited him to come to Panama to review our system and make a recommendation. I liked Percy from the minute I met him. He really knew his stuff, and I got the sense pretty quickly that if we were going to be a successful telephone sportsbook that relied on the latest phone technology, we needed a Percy on our team full-time.

One thing I really liked about Percy was that from our very first technical meeting he referred to the company as "us" or "we." He would say:

"*We* need to have diagnostic software running all the time."

"That will help *us* to head off any problems before they are unfixable."

He acted as if he were a full-time employee even before we hired him.

Percy was instrumental in helping us decide to move our base of operation from Panama to the technologically advanced environment that Costa Rica had to offer. I remember thinking to myself, *If there are guys like Percy and William in Costa Rica, a short flight away, what the hell am I doing in a backward and oppressive country like Panama?*

Percy spoke a mile a minute—his mouth could barely keep up with his brain. He would start and end every sentence with the phrase "mae, mae, mae" (pronounced "my my, my"). It is a Costa Rican phrase that means "Hey, man." He'd ask, "Mae, mae, mae, you want some coffee, mae?"

That was just the way he talked, and we all accepted it as a side effect of his genius. Percy was truly a technological genius so far ahead of the pack that I offered him a job as my head telephone tech for $50,000 a year, three times as much as the local telephone company was paying him to run the international phone department.

Percy relished the opportunity to build our phone operation. I was never sure if he did so because of the money or the challenge of building a telephone system of the future, from scratch, with no real budgetary issues. You see, the equipment at the local phone company, although revolutionary compared to Panama, was actually antiquated and limited in its scope. With our system and our funding, Percy could put to work all of the ideas he had been pondering for the last fourteen months.

Percy was the type of guy who used the Internet via a modem between his cell phone and his laptop, in his car, while he was driving. This is the type of thing that most techs don't do even today, ten years later. He would routinely log into our system from the road to make sure it was running properly.

I remember him sitting down with me before leaving to go back to Costa Rica. He said he would love to work for me, but Panama just didn't have the technological infrastructure to make it worthwhile to us to hire him. He said it would be like hiring a top surgeon, only to tie his hands before surgery. When I looked into his eyes, he gave me the same type of confidence that William Ramirez gave me. I felt I had finally found the missing link.

Remember, the phones were the most important aspect of our business. Without functioning phones, we were finished. Without a better option on the table, I took Percy's advice and we planned to immediately move our whole operation to Costa Rica.

Percy wasn't the most handsome guy. He had bad acne and an afro. As a white man, that wasn't the best look for him. But what he didn't have in looks he made up for in integrity and desire. Percy was a perfectionist who took even one minute of phone downtime personally, as if he were to blame. This was in stark contrast to the blame game we always got in Panama.

Percy was a diamond in the rough, and just what we needed to propel ourselves to the next level. We joined forces and never looked back. Once we decided to set up shop in Costa Rica, Percy became our "phone guy."

Percy immediately went to work on setting us up. Not only

was I dreaming big, but so was he. He suggested that rather than deal with the local phone company in Costa Rica, we avoid relying on any outside source for any services by installing our own satellite and monster PBX and managing our own signal. With Percy in charge, all of this was possible. By the time he had our phones up in Costa Rica, thirty days prior to deadline, our phones sounded like we were talking from the States. There were none of the serious echo or volume problems we had experienced in Panama. The customers loved it and stopped complaining about phone quality. This was the biggest step we had taken as a company since we swapped Brian for William.

In coordinating the laying of two fiber-optic lines (one was a backup) and solving our phone problems, Percy wound up putting Costa Rica on the map as the telephone call center capital of Central America.

My father was still the lines maker from Florida. Sandy ran the customer service department, and I was the conductor, guiding a two-hundred-person bookmaking orchestra. Costa Rica, with its educated workforce, saw in us a technologically advanced business that would provide good jobs and economic growth for its citizens. Since our business created jobs locally and brought in international commerce, we were the same kind of dream come true for Costa Rica as it was for us.

Percy got the ICE to approve us for our own "bird." A bird is the same satellite that the phone company uses to land its signals. Needless to say, after receiving a lot of assurances and spending $500,000, we never had phone problems again. Percy and the other Costa Ricans we dealt with were all up front, which was a nice change from every Panamanian we dealt with who had his own agenda and was looking to line his own pockets. Percy even explained how he could set up the system for us. He showed us the big building that would eventually become our headquarters. I was breathless. It looked like an airplane hangar. I had come from small backrooms in New York and a little two-thousand-square-foot office in a bank building in Panama. This was tens of thousands of square feet. You could fit a football field in this hangar. Looking across this new landscape, I saw my vision more clearly than ever. I envisioned the booths, all two hundred of them. I heard the phones ringing. I saw the dream.

The dream became reality in my head: No longer would bookmaking be confined to back rooms and basements in Brooklyn. I'd turn bookmaking into something like a New York Stock Exchange–traded company, a *Fortune* 500 business—the biggest of its kind in the entire world. I had already, by starting credit card betting and going offshore, changed the way the business was conducted. Now I'd take it to new heights—unbelievable heights and, for others, unforeseeable heights. I knew from the ads we had run with Stu Feiner that we had a monster just waiting to be unleashed. As far as I was concerned, and from everything I saw, Costa Rica had everything we needed.

With millions invested by New York already and millions more needed, I knew the dream I had sold everyone had better become a reality soon, or they would find me at the bottom of shit's creek with a paddle lodged up my ass.

I called my wife and told her about the beautiful home I was going to have waiting for her and our unborn child. I called New York to get more money, and they were behind me 100 percent. They totally bought into the dream I was pushing. After a full day of exploring Costa Rica, Sandy, William, Percy, and I headed back to the hotel. We were partying like crazy, drinking champagne—but more than the champagne it was the feeling and emotion that made us high. We were ecstatic, out of our minds. Life had never been this good, and the thing was, it was only going to get better. I remember choking back tears at the mere thought of what was about to happen.

And then the phone rang. I remember saying to myself, *This can't be good.* It felt like a theme to a movie I was making. Every time we were at our highest point, we got a fork in the friggin' eyes.

I picked up the phone thinking, *What the fuck is it now?* It was Luis, the chauffeur, on the line. Every local person we worked with in Panama was a spy for Sunny, and we knew that. Luis wasn't—he was loyal to us and liked us. We tipped him well, and we knew Sunny didn't give him a dime. Treating people right went a long way for us with everyone, and Luis was no exception.

I couldn't hear Luis at all with all the euphoria in the background.

"Everyone shut the fuck up for one second!" I pleaded. "I have to hear this call."

"Stevo, they have come and taken over the office and seized all the money," Luis spat out in a panic, sounding like he was choking for air. "The Salas brothers say they know you are leaving, and they have seized everything."

The party mood turned into a wake. All the noise went silent as I relayed what Luis had said. I've never experienced such an instantaneous swing of emotion in my entire life, and pray that I never will again. We had millions in customer money in our accounts. We had told everyone in the office we were just going to Costa Rica to look at acquiring a new credit card processor, but they obviously sensed what was going on.

They reacted in the only way their culture knows how—with hostility and rash action. That was just the way it worked in Panama. The Salas family (who ran the country's Supreme Court) and Sunny's people had taken over our office.

I thanked God my wife and unborn child were safe in Florida.

9

Playing with Fire:
Burning the Bridges to Panama

WE WERE SAFE in Costa Rica, but we had to deal with what would turn out to be a defining moment for us. With the bad news from Panama, the air went out of our balloon, and we all crashed emotionally.

We talked about what we were going to do next. I sat everyone down and gave them the halftime speech of my life. In this moment I knew I had to be the best salesman ever, rally the troops, point out that we had found a new paradise, and get us back on track. We had shown up in shithole Panama in June and had a company running profitably by September. I told everyone in the room that we could do it again, and that without all the bullshit in Panama only the sky would be the limit in Costa Rica.

I called Ray Salas in Panama.

"What's going on?" I asked Ray.

"Why don't you tell me?" Ray answered. "I heard you're opening a bookmaking business in Costa Rica."

"No, that's crazy," I said.

"You come back, and we'll talk," Ray said.

"Listen, there is no way I'm going to come back," I said. "I don't feel safe. What you did was a hostile act, and now I have to consider my options."

That put them on notice that I wasn't about to cave in and give them their way. They did have millions of ours frozen, but I quickly found out from our lawyers that they couldn't take it from us—they could freeze it, sure, but they didn't have the authority or means to take the money. That would eventually give us the wiggle room we needed to negotiate a settlement.

I went back to the U.S. and met with Bo and Donnie in Brooklyn and let them know what was going on.

My father, as he has always done my whole life, stepped up and used some cards he had stashed up his sleeve to help shape and secure our destiny.

I RETURNED TO Costa Rica to get the new business up and running while the drama unfolded in Panama. We brought our best employees from Panama over, notably William Ramirez, Eduardo Herrera, and Alberto Moke.

I tried to get Panamanian lawyers to go with my father to the meeting he had set up with the Salas brothers in Panama City, but no Panamanian lawyer would touch us. Word had gotten out, and they would not fight the government because they knew what would happen to them in later cases if they faced Judge Salas.

I really thought I needed to be in Panama with my dad.

"Stevo, go open your new business in Costa Rica, and leave this Panama problem to me," my father told me. "I will take care of everything. Trust me!"

My dad flew in and met Sandy, who had immediately returned to Panama to close out all of our personal affairs.

My dad and Sandy were about to enter into negotiations with the corrupt Panamanian government officials and businessmen without any leverage, security, or guarantees.

Or so I thought.

Sunny's wife, Chi-Chi (pronounced "chee-chee"), lived in Miami. While my dad refuses to admit it, I believe that "arrangements" were made with regard to Sunny's wife. A sort of "insurance policy" had been put in place back in Miami. In fact, I wouldn't be surprised if she sat tied to a chair in her apartment, awaiting word of my dad's fate—and her subsequent freedom.

My father landed in Panama and was met by Sandy, who was extremely anxious for him to arrive, as you can imagine. That said, Sandy always exhibited extreme courage and willingness to do whatever it took for the team. While we didn't always see eye to eye on policy, politics, and life strategy, I truly admired him for the way he handled himself in the line of fire. He was more than my general manager: he was my best friend, and is still to this day.

At that point, we still had several other bank accounts that Sunny and Salas didn't know about and so hadn't frozen. While he waited for my dad to come in for the meeting, Sandy went running from bank to bank, withdrawing all the money he could in cash, looking over his shoulder, changing cabs two and three times, and hiding the money under the septic tank at his home. He had been a public defender in Miami ten months earlier, and now it was like he was the protagonist of a John Grisham novel—getting all he could before the bad guys got to him. He had more than $450,000 squirreled away by the time my dad arrived in Panama for the meeting.

At the airport, when my dad saw Sandy, who was visibly shaken, he gave him a big hug and whispered, "Sandy, there is nothing to fear, everything is going to be fine."

Sandy remembers my father then pulling aside Sunny, who had shown up at the airport as well, and whispering something to him. He then handed Sunny a note that I would later find out was written by his wife Chi-Chi back in Miami.

"Sunny turned white as milk," Sandy said. "If he didn't piss his pants, I'd be shocked."

Whatever message was conveyed in that note seemed to give my dad all the leverage he would need to stay safe and unharmed during the entire negotiation process. Chi-Chi was fucked if Sunny pulled anything, and he knew it.

I should have realized that my father never would have agreed to play in a game that he wasn't fixing. He only plays when he is holding all the cards. He always said that the best poker players aren't the ones with the most skill but the ones who make the most money playing, and that comes from choosing your opponents wisely and leaving nothing up to luck. He would have never made that trip without any leverage.

Sometimes when the guys you are playing with want to take you to the mat, you have to hit them first, and hit them harder. That might mean hitting them when they aren't looking. Tough shit. They'd have done the same thing to you if they could have. My dad was smarter and tougher and had bigger balls than all of them combined.

Because he'd been a bookmaking client of ours for years and years, Sunny knew my father didn't dick around when it came to these things. Sunny was related to the president of Panama at the time and enjoyed the full power of the royal family, but in one swift move my dad had him right where he wanted him, no different than when he hustled cards as a Brooklyn youth. You could be the most skilled cardplayer in the world, but if my dad put in a cold deck you were going down. And the bigger they were, the harder they fell.

Sunny drove Sandy and my father to the meeting in his car. Once they got there, Sunny pulled Ray aside for a few minutes. While I don't know the exact words he used, I have an idea he said something to the effect that they couldn't play hardball as they intended. The evidence is to follow.

The Panamanians had brought our business, and theirs, to its knees by freezing our money and taking over our building. The hardest part for me was that I couldn't get money to my customers, which was my trademark on the streets. Not to mention that the delayed payments would hurt us in our new operation as we tried to get that up and running. We needed a resolution, and we needed it that day. While Sunny and Ray were assholes, they weren't idiots. They knew that the business I had started was the dawning of a new era and that the seeds for that era had been planted in their country. But neither of these guys was extraordinarily bright, either. And both were greedy fuckers who lived only in the moment.

The meeting got under way at the Salas law offices in a beautiful, luxurious building in Panama City.

My dad and Sandy, without legal representation, faced Sunny, Ray, and their eight Panamanian top-gun lawyers, as well as several current or former top government ministers, with Ray Salas's father, the Supreme Court justice, on speakerphone and me listening in as well via Sandy's cell phone in his pocket. These lawyers Sunny and Ray had weren't just local guys. Several had gone to Harvard or other Ivy League law schools and returned to their home country to set up practice or work for the government. They were top dogs.

My dad ran the show from the opening bell. He started the meeting with the following statement:

"I just want to say a few words before we get started here. I'm not a lawyer or a government official. I came to this meeting in good faith, amid obvious concerns for my personal safety and security. While I am hopeful that this meeting will not get ugly, I just want to go on record in case it does. I respect your power and position in the place that I am currently standing. However, I just want to remind you that back in Miami my people stand with more power and an extremely superior position to yours. If anything were to happen to Sandy or me, my people are prepared to do what is necessary. You all travel through Miami. It is the hub for American Airlines International, and all flights from Panama go through there. I promise that I will treat you with the same respect, and grant you the same liberties on my streets, that I am afforded here on yours."

There was silence for a good ninety seconds as my dad sat back in his chair and sipped his coffee. It must have felt like ten minutes to those people in the room. Hell, it seemed like an hour to me on the phone, but I couldn't help but smile because I knew the hand my dad was playing, and my old man was playing it perfectly.

Sunny, whose wife would be the first one to lose, jumped up from his seat and assured my dad that this was a peaceful negotiation to resolve the matter at hand.

"Dave, we understand what you are saying, and there isn't going to be any fucking funny business here, I assure you," Sunny said. "Please, let's get started with the meeting, okay?"

Sunny was drunk—he was always drunk. He drank more before 10:00 AM than most people drank all day and night. He usually handled himself pretty well, but that day he was shaky at best.

The Panamanians started talking in circles, grandstanding, saying nothing of substance. Sandy added his two cents occasionally. Accusations flew, and the Panamanians hinted at veiled threats, which always led to Sunny jumping up and putting out the fire before it started to burn out of control.

Finally, when the meeting had gone on for two hours without going anywhere significant, Supreme Court Justice Salas spoke up from the speakerphone.

"We have had your business assessed at $30 million," Justice Salas said. "I will take $5 million for our 15 percent interest in your business, and you can go back to work here with 100 percent ownership—you can buy us out."

A pause. The ball was in our court, and I knew it. My old man was ready to take away the fucking ball and shut down these assholes' court so they couldn't play anymore. Game on. My dad was playing poker against a bunch of suckers.

"I agree with your $30 million figure—in fact, that might even be a little low," my father said. I was shocked. Was my dad considering paying these thieving rat bastards $5 million? I listened intently as he continued. "With that as your own measuring stick, though, I will offer you a better deal. I will agree to give you our 85 percent of the business for that same $5 million. By your own figures, that's a dream deal for you, and I will leave my son's supervisors here for two months to train your guys on how to run your operation. Deal?"

The Panamanians were flabbergasted. My dad had already won, and they were just figuring it out. There were some more harsh exchanges. Again a drunk Sunny was responsible for jumping in between any potential face-off.

Through it all, my father kept negotiating. He knew that they were desperate and that they couldn't steal the money from the bank, so he made them this "final offer."

"You keep the entire business, all the equipment and furniture, and keep running it, and we'll give you $50,000 to unfreeze our money and let us leave," Dad said.

The Panamanians jumped at the bait. The Salas family, although politically powerful, was of modest and humble roots. We knew Sunny was broke from gambling. $50K was too much for them to pass up, as that was double their yearly income. On the other hand, that same amount was peanuts for us to give up as a "moving expense," especially compared to the amount that was frozen.

They would make a futile attempt to run the bookmaking business on their own. The problem was that no one knew a damn thing about running the business, plus they were all so corrupt that they started stealing from each other almost immediately. It was like handing the cheese to the rats: They ate it before they were out the door and wondered what happened the next day when everything was gone.

After my father made his "final offer," Sunny stood up.

"Done!" Sunny said. "Let's all shake hands and go."

"Wait!" Justice Salas shouted over the speakerphone. "Those trucks they have, I want them."

"The trucks?" Sunny asked.

"The Land Rovers, the black one and the green one. I want them—or the deal is off," Salas said.

Sandy slid the keys across the table. We did insist on keeping ownership of our company phone number, and they agreed. So, for $50,000 and two Land Rovers that we couldn't take with us to Costa Rica anyway, my dad and Sandy were able to fly out that night on a private plane from Panama, with Sandy carrying a briefcase full of the cash that he had emptied out of the several hidden bank accounts Sunny and his crew never knew about.

They unfroze our money, and we got it via bank wire immediately. The first thing I did was pay off our customers and set up a hotline for them to call and get updates on the progress and opening of the new place in Costa Rica. We had the phone number of our old office switched to a recording announcing that we were expanding and moving to a new office in beautiful Costa Rica. The transition to Costa Rica had successfully begun, and while the road ahead was uncertain, that was nothing new for me by this point.

What started out as a $5 million shakedown, ended up a mere $50k exit fee. My father, who I idolized, who I had seen accomplish amazing things throughout my whole life, and who had always come through for me in the past, had saved his best performance for last.

And I had never needed it more.

10

Putting Together a Winning Lineup

FOLLOWING OUR EXODUS from Panama, but before we set up
shop in Costa Rica, my father went to New York to sit down
with Bo and Donnie. They were our New York backers, muscle, and silent partners from the very start. These were two of
the most established bookmakers/bettors in the business. While
I have no doubt that they appreciated my overall mission to
take bookmaking mainstream, they were in it to make money,
not to pioneer an industry. These were old-school, in-your-face
guys. Bo and Donnie were the kind of guys who, in running
bookmaking operations in New York, had fully mastered the
techniques of risk versus reward. To them, this was an investment, and according to what I had told them—and what they
had invested in me—it had better be a blue-chipper.

My dad had to personally go explain the situation to Bo and
Donnie, and more importantly, get the final approval for the
extra funding we needed to launch the Costa Rican operation
in time for football season, which was just sixty days away. The
bottom line was that if we weren't up and running for football
season, we'd be screwed.

I decided to relocate my twenty best employees from Panama to Costa Rica to give me speed to market, quality assurance, and experienced trainers I could rely on to teach the Costa Ricans my way of operating a bookmaking business.

The crew we brought from Panama to Costa Rica included the following key personnel:

Eduardo Herrera was our head bookmaker who replaced Howie the spy in Panama as boss of the bookmaking department. He was an ex–Noriega army lieutenant, but as honest as he was loyal. He was also a tough son of a bitch, and to this day we remain close friends. He became like a brother to me over time as we weathered many storms together. In Costa Rica he would shine and later become a bookmaking legend highly revered among Costa Rican bookmakers, and he remains among the best in the game today.

Jami Uriola, who would later become Eduardo's wife, ran the credit card security department for us. She had started out as an entry-level clerk on the B shift—exactly as Eduardo had. Jami had gained infamous status for making a five-figure fuck-up on her first night working. She took the following "if" bet: $40,000 on the Miami Dolphins -6, if they win, a $40,000 parlay on Dolphins -6 and the Dolphins over 41. It was a classic example of a pro taking advantage of a rookie clerk. You obviously can't make an "if" bet off of a winner to a parlay with the same team in it, which would be a huge advantage to the player. That would be like going to the horse track and saying, "If the horse Lucky Shoes wins in the first race, I want to bet him in the daily double for the next race." No way: You have to do the two races before the first race is run. But that's the bet she took, and since she worked for me, it was my mistake and I had to rectify it. I got the customer on the phone and said it was our mistake. I gave him a $1,000 free cash bonus and eliminated the "illegal" bet.

That $1,000 saved me more money down the line, because while it was an honest mistake on Jami's part, that jerk-off spy Howie was right there and still with us when it happened. That was the beginning of the end for him. You don't let a clerk write a $40,000 bet on her first night, period, much less let it go unsupervised. It was bad enough that Howie was a spy. What made things worse was that he was an incompetent head clerk.

Javier Pena ran the bookmaking department for Eduardo during the off hours and was Eduardo's top dog during the rush hours. Javier was a trouper, a real company man. But he loved wounded women. If a girl had a limp or a deformity, he was all over her. He wasn't that bad-looking either, but like a wild animal in the jungle, when he sensed weakness in his prey, he pounced. He wound up marrying a woman with a debilitating bone defect that caused her a lot of pain and discomfort whenever she walked, and they lived happily ever after.

I found Gabi Mitchell at the local cable company in Panama. She sold me an upgrade to my system. I enticed her to leave the cable office with me that same day and come to work— that very same day—for me. She was a heavyset, sexy Latina woman, and she knew how to work it. She became a staple in our customer service department in Costa Rica and is still working at a top level in the industry today.

Arturo was a funny guy, worth having around just for the feeling his smiles gave you. But he was also a complete, raving alcoholic, so we had to keep an eye on him. Arturo had been a big-time radio personality in Panama. He spoke English so well that we just had to take him. He later became the John Belushi of the *Animal House*–like dorm setting in Costa Rica where all the clerks lived. Although he turned out to be the life of the party, we eventually had to get rid of him before he killed himself—and whoever was caught under his four-hundred-pound body when he passed out.

Ayana was my personal secretary, and worth her weight in gold. She was on top of things and was an excellent communicator. Loyal. She knew the inside scoop on me and in some cases had more info than even my wife did. Our relations were not physical at all; she took care of everything for me and handled herself with the class and dignity that you would expect from the boss's number-one secretary. She looked a little bit like Mary J. Blige, which is nice, but not my taste. Howie the scumbag spy, on the other hand, loved her and every other black woman he could get his hands on. A white Jew from Brooklyn, Howie might have more black kids than Evander Holyfield.

Lizbeth was Sandy's personal secretary—his Ayana, if you will. Lizbeth was extremely smart and all business all the time. She later went on to run the accounting department under Javier Camacho, and she was invaluable. She looked a little like Snuffleupagus from *Sesame Street,* though, and she always had about 45 snot-filled tissues crumpled up all around her. She had a cold 365 days a year, yet she never missed a single day of work.

Alberto Moke was the chief organizer of whatever needed to get done locally in Panama, then in Costa Rica. He put together all the corporate events and stockpiled them with the best hookers around, age twenty-one and under. He also excelled at anything that required local dealmaking and negotiations. He was a Ferenge, if you follow *Star Trek*—a big-time dealmaker. Everyone, even those he hustled, loved him. You couldn't help but love this guy.

Jose Cernuda was another top employee and a really loyal guy. The problem was that he spoke like he had marbles in his mouth, so nobody could ever really confirm one thing that he ever said. He was a really smart guy, but ironically he spoke Spanish, his native language, even worse than he spoke English. Listening to him was like listening to someone speaking underwater. He worked with "internal affairs"—which is to say, within the office. To that end, he was a great assistant for Eduardo and a top trainer, too, but he was never allowed to speak with a customer. Ever. He did have a sister, Viviana, who was astoundingly attractive, so I had to hire her as a personal secretary just so I could look at her ass all day. One day at the office in Costa Rica she raised her arms and I saw the hairiest armpits I'd seen in my life, so I transferred her to the other side of the office where Sandy worked.

Oscar Zefferin was another character we loved. He was a cross between Billy Dee Williams and LL Cool J. He brought a slick voice to customer service and became a supervisor in Costa Rica.

I also took some other clerks, customer service reps, and specialty secretaries I just couldn't live without, if you know what I mean. These Panamanians had never been out of Panama before, so this was the chance of a lifetime for them, and they all responded with tremendous passion, effort, and teamwork. Without these loyal Panamanian employees, we would not have opened in time in Costa Rica or been able to run the day-to-day operations with the same flawless execution that our customers were already accustomed to.

While my father was meeting with Bo and Donnie, I was working the phones and lining up backup investors. I remember getting the call from my dad about 2:00 AM telling me that

Bo and Donnie were in, but that the stakes were at an all-time high. They were in for whatever it took and were hell-bent on getting their entire investment back plus profits as soon as possible. They knew about the late surge we'd had in Panama, and they realized we were sitting on a potential giant. I guess it was ultimately their greed combined with their belief in my dad's past and my future that kept them at the table. They knew that if I could iron out all the wrinkles, I could take them to the moon and back. And if I failed, well, there would be a price to pay for that, too, and my father informed me as much.

"Stevie, this is it," Dad said. "They ain't going for another fucking penny after this, so you better take your best shot here. They're not thrilled, but they're in. Look, son, I went to bat for you here because I believe in you, but if you crap out, you better fucking disappear, okay?"

There would be no failing this time because failure wasn't an option I was even entertaining. In fact, I was never so sure of anything in my life, despite the many what-ifs on the horizon. Going into Panama, I hadn't known what to expect. I had been optimistic in the face of total uncertainty, even playing against a stacked deck with Sonny, Salas, and the rest of those money-grubbing pricks. But going into Costa Rica, we were already established, and there was no need to use my imagination to see where this was headed.

Becoming a monster would bring other concerns, like how to deal with blowing the ceiling off the gambling world and dealing with tens of millions—even hundreds of millions—of dollars in profits, while potentially upsetting the powers-that-be in both the underworld and the U.S. government. This was when I hired Paul Pringles as my security adviser. He was recommended to me by my Miami attorneys at the time. I met with

Pringles in Costa Rica, and he sold me on the fact that as a retired FBI agent whose girlfriend was still an active FBI agent, he could always keep his finger on the pulse and gauge what the current mood of the FBI was as it related to pursuing and investigating offshore gambling. I knew this would be an important component to our future strategy, so I hired him. I'd seen how the business exploded in Panama, and I knew that the potential for us in Costa Rica was unlimited. That kind of success could become a headache, but I was willing to deal with a lot worse than a headache to get what I wanted.

11

A Little Bit of Heaven
and a Hell of a Lot of Money

COSTA RICA WAS an ultra-friendly country compared to Panama, a little paradise, tucked away and special. Then again, after living in Panama for almost a year, the South Side of Chicago would have seemed like an upgrade. There was no time to party, but we always found time anyway. Still, I had precious little time to get my new Costa Rican operation open before I'd lose my old clients to another sportsbook for football season.

Other offshore bookmaking operations had followed our lead and started sprouting up and siphoning off bettors from the United States, the main market. Thankfully, many of those new companies were underfunded, inexperienced, and simply ill equipped to compete with me. I made sure that above all else, my clients were always paid immediately. At the end of the day, paying my customers fast was the best marketing money that I could spend because that was what customers were most concerned with and that was what made them recommend their friends to us. If they won $100 or $10,000, it didn't mean shit to them if they had to wait weeks or months to get paid.

That is why I paid more than a million dollars, when I left Panama, to my clients, who would have had no recourse had I decided to steal it. That was money I could have used to build our Costa Rican operation instead of putting my life on the line with Bo and Donnie by having them press their bets and up their ante. I knew that paying the money would ultimately earn me more value going forward than a quick pop from a snatch-and-grab. Besides, it wasn't my money, and I wasn't a thief. Little did I know that I was once again crossing a threshold, with the fate of an entire industry on my back. Had I decided to rob that money, the industry as a whole would have fallen.

At that time, the million-plus on deposit I sent back was a huge amount because it was after the football season and it represented only about 30 percent of the customer base. Most guys in my position would have pocketed the money and used it to open up shop in Costa Rica under an assumed name not connected in any way to the company that had stolen it.

I remember my dad weighing in and assuring me that there was no decision to be made, and that sending everyone back their money was the only choice for me.

"Son, there was a time in my life, in my youth, when I would have taken this money and never looked back," my father said. "However, you have created something bigger than anything I could have ever hustled up. Don't ruin it all with an act of greed and stupidity."

He was right, as usual, and I knew it. I saw the real value of staying true to my core beliefs and further strengthening my name-brand recognition with my clients—and with Bo and Donnie, too. Besides, I was always a big believer in the karmic factor: In my line of work you just don't do those types of things and live to tell about them. And you don't get greedy when you have a license to steal, which is what we had in Panama and, in effect, in Costa Rica.

This strategy worked like a charm when September rolled around because the freshest memories in the minds of my customers were the checks they received when we closed up shop in Panama and how unbelievably honest we were. The bookmaking business is shady by definition, and it had only grown murkier as my competition copied our ideas but never our commitment to paying customers. On their part, that was extremely shortsighted.

None of my customers from Panama had expected to get paid; they were all shocked to receive their money via FedEx. Along with their checks was a toll-free information line that would eventually become our new phone number in Costa Rica, 1-888-Bet-Easy. Oddly enough, that number is still in use today by the cousins of P-Man the Greek, who bought me out after I got pinched.

I sent a letter to all the customers, along with their checks, explaining that I had decided to move our base of operations from Panama to Costa Rica in order to upgrade our technical infrastructure and better accommodate our clients' needs. The true "technical" problem with Panama was that I couldn't live one day longer in that under-evolved, Third World, oppressive rat hole, much less spend another football season there.

Wouldn't you know it—the day after we sent out the checks our new number received several thousand calls. We used this line to update our status and plans every single day and to give our customers a way to keep in touch with us. Betting customers are obsessive by nature, and that phone number with the daily progress update and countdown to launch was their security blanket; it helped ease what otherwise could have been an uncomfortable transition. Remember, we were a bookmaking operation, not IBM, but nevertheless customers really enjoyed having their hands held. No one in my field had ever done business like me, and the fact that our clients had tangible proof that we cared about them was a huge ace up our sleeve. We would need that ace, as we were getting ready to deal the world a whole new hand.

Since we were no longer the only ones in the world taking offshore bets, customer retention had to be our priority. And the way we built trust with our customers was not simply a turning point for my own company but a moment of truth for the entire industry. I had to lay the foundation of trust on which the entire industry depended. That process made believers out of people who were extremely wary of offshore betting. As we got closer to opening in Costa Rica, we found that not only had we retained nearly our entire customer base, but also that word of our honesty and integrity had spread and our reputation and customer base had spread along with it. All the trust that I gained from paying the thousands of bettors back their money had allowed this newly born industry to continue breathing during its darkest hour, and then ultimately flourish. Paying all my clients upon leaving Panama was what officially confirmed the new offshore sportsbook industry as legitimate, and me as its father.

Costa Rica was a perfect fit for my company, as it gave us all the physical resources we needed and a stress-free environment. The move also renewed my passion for the dream I had—the dream of building the biggest bookmaking operation the world had ever seen.

Change was coming, and not just for my company but for me personally. I had overcome a treacherous, onerous situation in

Panama and landed not just on my feet but in a position to take the industry to a whole new level. I had paid my dues on the streets of Miami, survived Panama despite long odds, and kept my credibility and integrity intact throughout.

Costa Rica also saw me step completely out of my father's shadow and become the boss of the family business. It was a changing of the guard that was a long time coming. My dad couldn't have been prouder, though, and more willing to step aside. He was teaching me again, teaching me how love is stronger than ego. He had worked his whole life to get me to this point, and I was ready and up to the task. I changed the name of the business from International Sports Club to SDB (my initials, Steven Darren Budin) Global. I felt invincible, and for the first time ever I was widely regarded throughout the industry as the kingpin, a role I really cherished.

I rented a small twenty-five-room hillside hotel in the downtown San Jose area and made it the "dorm" for my Panamanian exiles. These folks, who knew how to party, found that, in stark contrast to the oppression of Panama, independent thought was the norm in the democracy of Costa Rica. They lived it up, and every night was a fiesta. They celebrated the good life in this beautiful new country, which was only a short plane ride but really a world away from Panama. I harnessed that good vibe and got every ounce of effort from them on the job. But working for SDB Global was so much more than a job—we were like a family.

Once outfitted with the latest technology, the huge Allajuela-based office space in the SARET free trade zone, which had previously been a shrimp factory, went from looking like an empty airplane hangar to the main deck of the *Starship Enterprise*. We started training Costa Rican employees in our makeshift classrooms. The Panamanians I brought turned out to be even better teachers than they had been students, and that allowed Sandy, William, Eduardo, and me to work on the bigger-picture issues.

We were running what looked like a junior college from morning until night. We taught American sports betting, the English language, and the culture of the betting world. We had Costa Rican employees who were educated, well spoken, well groomed, and respectful. They learned on an astonishingly steep curve and mastered even complex matters through hours of studying and practice.

When it was close to launch time, we started with twenty-four phone lines, a number that would double within four months. That was a far cry from the eight lines we had started with in Panama. I was in the flow, and everyone around me was motivated by my desire to achieve my goals through hard work, dedication, experience, and balls of steel. My Panamanians had seen what I had endured and overcome in their country. So that group especially saw the greatness on the horizon for us in Costa Rica.

Our corporate culture, which grew the business by leaps and bounds, was mainly reflected in how we treated our staff and how they in turn treated our customers. We were better than anyone else offshore and did far more volume than anyone on American soil. Most bookies were harsh and rash. Our tone was polite, courteous, and pleasant. Local bookies still wrote by hand and made mistakes. We worked on computers, so we were always accurate. These things all added that corporate touch to the whole experience. We didn't offer credit, the bane of many local bookmakers, but we did take credit cards. We paid our clients seven days a week, not just once a week, as local bookies did.

So it evolved that I wasn't even competing with local bookies. We offered a service that they could not, from the technology down to our customer service and, most importantly, our payment practices. I wanted the "little" gambler betting a few hundred instead of $50, and I wanted the big bettors raising it to several hundred thousand. We took $250,000 bets on single games, and word of that spread like wildfire. Pretty soon everyone in the world knew we took the biggest bets. To the gamblers, that was a major credibility issue, and bigger did mean better because it meant that if we could handle the whales, the guppies had no concerns. This enhanced both our reputation and our mystique.

When I walked through the office, it was like being onstage. It was rock & roll from the second I hit the building every day. I was shaping my young, adoring, and impressionable employees into tomorrow's bookies and leading by example. That was familiar territory to me because of my experiences on the many South Beach stages I had rocked in the early '90s as lead singer and rapper in the band STEVO (of course). We were the Sunday night house band in the famous Talkhouse on Sixth and Collins on South Beach. The Talkhouse had been South Beach's most formidable live rock venue ever. Back then, I was a bookmaker by day and a rock rapper by night. It was an odd combination, but a great cover for me if nothing else. At the pinnacle of my rock & roll moment, I opened up for the Counting Crows in Fort Lauderdale at an unbelievable outdoor venue called The Edge. I remember doing acid for the first time that night with the band and coming just short of a religious experience musically. In fact, we had been asked to go on a college tour the same week I was slated to move to Panama. I was tempted to pursue a career in music, but my true love was separating suckers from their money.

So after three years and two CDs, including the release of a single and a video on MTV's *Video Jukebox,* I chose to pursue the obtainable dream, which meant putting down my childhood toys and doing what I was best at. That decision ultimately landed me in the hell that was Panama—and then the paradise that was, and is, Costa Rica.

I make the musical analogy because the high I experienced onstage with all eyes on me was exactly what I felt in Costa Rica when I was moving the company forward on my shoulders. The whole company was in sync like a band—in the pocket and grooving our way toward becoming the biggest bookmaking operation ever seen. The office was my stage, and every move I made was watched by our three hundred employees with the same focus and intensity I'd felt from the fans who had gathered each Sunday night at the Talkhouse on South Beach to watch me rock the house, time and time again, without failure and without flaw.

Bets, drugs, and rock & roll.

12

Life in the Fast Lane, Dodging Potholes Left and Right

DESPITE THE WONDERFUL surroundings and people, the start-up in Costa Rica was ten times harder and more intense than our original start-up in Panama. There was so much riding on this one, and the pressure was intense.

Existing clients were itching to play again, and new clients were ready to be swallowed up by the new companies that started to pop up left and right. I also had New York breathing down my neck to get open and to start getting them back some of their many millions, so I spent the first three months working fifteen-hour days and collapsing when I got home.

I had to outfit what looked like an empty airplane hangar with the latest technology and everything else it needed to function. Simultaneously, we were training new clerks and setting up our banking infrastructure. There was not much time for fun and games in those first ninety days, but eventually things settled down to a fast, but manageable, pace.

Pretty soon I was back to my old tricks again.

We had a special secretary pool in the back of the office, in a side room with no windows to the main office. We kept all the sexy secretaries back there, out of view, just in case any of the wives made a surprise visit. One girl, a nineteen-year-old new hire named Mimi, started frequenting my office, always making sure she was the one to bring me my morning faxes. I remember one day my wife was in Miami on an extended vacation and I was in my office in Costa Rica and in the mood for some fun. I called Mimi in from the back office and asked her to close the door behind her.

"What can I do for you, boss?" she demurred with puppy- dog eyes, her miniskirt barely covering her nineteen-year-old apple pie.

These were the temptations I faced on a daily basis there. I know it sounds like a scene from a cheap porno, but that was Costa Rica for you. The chicks were young and hot, and it was a man's world, especially when you were "the boss man."

I remember when my wife, six months pregnant, came back to Costa Rica after a month of visiting with her family in Florida and rushed to surprise me in the office. She ran past my receptionist and, before she could be stopped, barged into my office.

"Stevo, I'm back!" she yelled.

My desk chair, with its back to my wife, slowly swiveled around to expose the long legs and short skirt of Mimi, who was just hanging out in my chair and playing house in my office.

Mimi, not knowing the visitor was my wife, asked in a diva tone, "Mr. Budin is not here right now. Did you have an appointment? Can I help you?"

My wife, pregnant with our second child, took one look at Mimi and almost gave birth right then and there.

"Can you help me, you fucking whore? Yes, get your shit and get the fuck out of my husband's chair. You're fired!" my wife said.

Mimi, shocked and frightened, looked over to my receptionist at the door and said in Spanish, "Can she do that?"

My receptionist stood up from her desk, seized the opportunity to get on the good side of Mrs. B., and simply winked at my wife and said back in English, "That's Mrs. Budin, the boss's wife, and she can definitely do that. So go see Judy in accounting for your final check—now."

Luckily, I wasn't in the office to witness that exchange, but the welcome I did receive from my wife later that night at our Costa Rican home was more than memorable. All of my clothes were floating in the pool—$2,000 Italian suits soaking in the chlorine.

Before I could even say anything, I was dodging pots and pans and verbal assaults, all this while my pregnant wife was holding a cell phone to her ear, talking with her friend Jessica, Sandy's wife.

I finally calmed her down and explained that nothing happened between Mimi and me. My wife was a firecracker who wouldn't hesitate to clean house if she had to, and that's why I loved her. She didn't ever take any shit from me or anybody else.

OUR JOBS IN Costa Rica were very important jobs in the local economy, and by extension important to every local worker we employed.

To that end, our local employees would never put their jobs in jeopardy. We had gone the extra mile to keep our Costa Rican employees happy after the lessons we learned in Panama. Full disclosure here: In Panama I didn't know what the hell I was doing at times and would often scream at our employees, even about things that couldn't have been their fault. I just blew it in some cases with the way I handled our staff, though many times those explosions were born of frustration with how Panama's culture and shortcomings were failing us as a business.

I would always apologize after flying off the handle and wind up buying the entire office a pizza lunch, but I was clearly learning a lot from the on-the-job CEO training I was receiving. In Costa Rica I resolved to be a better boss, and as a result I did everything right comparatively. I was equally as strong, equally as demanding, without the need to ever apologize in front of the whole staff or buy pizza to make amends.

As in Panama, these young, well-educated people in Costa Rica had dream jobs working for us and were making far more money than they could make in the local business community. Working for us carried a local prestige, and our employees were visibly grateful.

During our first football season in Costa Rica, that bond with our employees really paid off, but not in a way that we had expected.

One day Carlos, a local employee, came to my office. I was talking to Sandy, and Carlos stood right at my door, pale-faced and sweating bullets. Kickoff for the early afternoon NFL games had just occurred, and we were all in a good mood. The money was rolling in, profits were through the roof, and we were all working hard. After the 1:00 PM kickoff, the shop would slow down to a crawl, and everyone would go outside on cigarette break, as there would be at least an hour's lull before the 4:00 games started to get any action. As in Panama, smoking cigarettes was the national pastime in Costa Rica, a weird juxtaposition in such a healthy, eco-friendly country.

A visibly nervous Carlos stood in my doorway, broken out in a cold sweat.

"What's wrong?" I asked him.

He was shaking.

"Just tell me," I instructed.

He shook his head no.

"Come with me," he said. "I'll show you, Mr. Stevo."

Carlos looked out the window to make sure his supervisor, Ben, was outside and had just lit his cigarette—an indication that he'd be outside for a few minutes. Ben was a local kid who had lived in New York City for ten years before moving back to Costa Rica and landing the gig with us, a gig that saw him rise quickly to the position of clerk supervisor.

Sandy and I followed Carlos to his workstation.

"Look at my computer," he said.

There was nothing strange at first glance.

Carlos sat down.

"I was sitting here, ready to take another bet, and Ben came by," Carlos said. He pointed to the bottom of his screen, where another window was still open but minimized and out of sight.

"Ben came by here," Carlos said quietly. "He opened up this window for another bet from a 1:00 PM game, left it open, and then minimized the screen. Ben said this was fine, he was doing a test. He told me not to worry about it. But I had to tell you and Mr. Sandy."

"Ben told you to leave the screen with the bet open?" I asked.

Carlos nodded yes.

"This is logged in as my name," Carlos said. "That's why I'm worried. He opened the window and pulled it down to where you cannot see it unless you know it's there. It's just . . ."

I'd heard enough. We walked back to my office. That little son of a bitch Ben had left a window open so he could fill in the winner after the game ended or when its outcome was obvious.

He had found a hole in our system, and I was pissed. In the software we had William write, he hadn't accounted for the program being open and running twice on one computer. Good ol' Ben had found a seam and was getting ready to exploit it.

"Go ahead back to your seat," I told Carlos. "You did the right thing. Go back to your seat, and don't worry. You're a good young man. We appreciate this."

"It's just . . . Señor Ben . . .," Carlos said.

"You are fine," I told Carlos. "I'll handle Ben. He's my problem now, not yours. Everything is cool as far as you are concerned. You did the right thing."

Carlos still looked scared, but followed the direction I gave him. Sandy and I went to the "fish tank" in the center of the room, and I called Eduardo and William over to us. Before Ben came back in, William confirmed that two programs were indeed running on Carlos's computer, meaning that Ben was trying to pull something on us. William closed the window immediately and deleted the ticket Ben had opened on Carlos's screen.

I had Ben paged over the PA system. We really liked Ben—he was an aggressive go-getter, a kid with some New York roots like myself, and he had all the smarts in the world.

And he's lucky it didn't get him killed.

We brought Ben to my office.

"You've got one fucking chance to tell me what's going on here," I told him as he started to shake. "And then it's going to get ugly."

We walked Ben out back, behind the building to an area that was surrounded by a thickly forested area. I'm certain Ben had no doubt that I might kill him, and I wanted to get all I could out of that fear—to confirm all the damage already done—but

I had zero intention of doing anything more than slapping him around a little. I was now running a company that had single-handedly brought an industry from the gutter to the mainstream, and I wasn't about to undo that by reacting as if we were operating on a Brooklyn street corner.

"I . . . yes," he said. "I had the one window open. But I just wanted to see if there was a hole in the program. I was planning to tell you guys or William right away."

"Fuck you," I said. "All I want to know is one thing, and you'd better think about this answer before you open your fucking mouth: Is this the first time you've done this?"

He was nodding yes before I finished the question.

"Yes, yes, absolutely yes," Ben answered. "I was going to find out and tell you. That's it. That's all. Nothing more. Never done it before. No way I'd mess with you. With you guys, no way. Please don't hurt me, please."

"Bullshit. You're fired," I said.

Ben nodded his head.

"I understand," he said. "But I'd just like to clean out my locker, and then I'll leave."

Sandy stood next to him, as I got right in his face.

"No way," I said. "You can't have anything out of your locker."

The little prick obviously had something of interest in his locker, and I was going to see exactly what that was.

"Get the fuck out of here," I said. "You're not even going back into the building. Walk around the outside of the building and leave. Never come back."

"Okay, okay, I understand," Ben said. "I'm gone. I'm out of here. Thank you for everything, Stevo. Even though I am fired, I understand and I love you guys!"

He was obviously feeling lucky to be alive.

A burly security guard of mine came out and joined us and walked Ben to his car.

When we got to Ben's locker a few minutes later, of course it turned out he had been lying to us. There we found a diary recording his every move. He had been doing this for three weeks and had "won" a little more than $15,000 fixing winners.

He had written it like a story in his diary, listing each game, how he had done it, what the payoff was. The key part was that he had even listed his user names and passwords and made them all the same—with a "WU" prefix—so that it was easy to track and also easy to close down. WU was short for "Western Union": He had opened his own account in New York and sent and received money through Western Union.

But there was more to the diary than that. Turns out he had gotten a local girl, one of our bet-taking clerks, pregnant. Ben was going a little insane. He wrote entries like, "Today, I will open a parlay for my unborn baby." At the end he listed exactly what he had siphoned, which of his "WU" accounts it had paid to, and closed with: "My baby is going to love me for WU."

Each of our accounts had two letters and four numbers; because of the "WU," we were able to find Ben's accounts immediately. Even without the "WU" we'd have been able to find his accounts because in the reams of pages in his diary he listed everything. We found sixteen accounts that he was using, all active.

We were actually quite fortunate that the incident with Ben happened: A 15k loss was bad, but it was peanuts compared to what he was planning and what he could have stolen from us in another month or so.

In fact, Ben saved us bigger money. Just two months later, we had a client who worked in Canada for the stock exchange in Toronto—the Canadian equivalent of the NYSE. We found more than twenty different accounts for this guy in Toronto, all with different credit card numbers and different names. We were able to cross-reference the credit cards because the two letters were the same on the account, and we gave the information to the Royal Canadian Mounted Police. They arrested the guy and sent him to prison. We caught this guy by using the suspicious activity software that William Ramirez created after the Ben incident.

I'm not saying, and would never say, that what Ben did was good. But I have to say this: I actually admired the kid. When you are a poor kid who's having a baby, you take some shots. Part of the game is taking shots, and he did it—albeit for a short while. I remember that Sandy and I looked at each other after we sent Ben on his way, and we were just smiling, thinking, *That little fucker Ben thought he could take us down.*

The kid had balls for trying to pull one over on me. That's part of the business. My father was the ultimate hustler, so a part of me couldn't help but admire the kid's guts. He was in the game and shot for the stars, and in the world of bets, drugs, and rock 'n' roll, that takes brass balls. On the streets, he would have caught a serious beating or worse, and rightfully so. How in the hell could I not have at least a little bit of respect for him? He wasn't hurting anyone. He viewed himself as Robin Hood, and he found a hole. Hell, if I, Sandy, William, and Eduardo were that much smarter than him, we would have found the hole first. Ben wasn't physically hurting anyone; he was just fudging a betting slip. But I couldn't let it slide, either. My reputation was on the line here. Without the proper response, it could have been open season for cheaters.

That's why they have cameras in Las Vegas—not to keep an

eye on the customers but on the staff. I had empathy for Ben—he had taken his chance. It only cost us $15,000 to close a hole in the program that could have—and would have—cost us hundreds of thousands, or even millions, if it had gone undetected.

Later I showed up at Ben's house with Sandy, his diary in my hands. He answered the door, and I hit him hard across the face with the book. He lay there on the floor shaking and crying.

"Ben, we're not done with you yet," I said. "I'd suggest you leave Costa Rica ASAP and go back to the Bronx where you have family—and where you might be safe. I know where you were sending the money—I have the address right here in my hand. I know where you are—I can reach out and grab you at any time."

Ben got on a plane that night and disappeared, never to return to Costa Rica.

Word spread back in our office that we had roughed up Ben pretty bad, even though I hadn't, and when he disappeared, other rumors started to swirl. Sometimes the rumor mill does some good. All anyone knew for sure was that Ben tried to fuck us and then disappeared, and that was a good thing.

Frankly, we were growing so fast—our clerks knew we were raking in more money than ever—that someone would have tried something sooner or later. But Ben getting caught put those thoughts out of everyone's mind. They didn't want to lose their jobs, or their lives. In this case, as in so many others in my life, I realized that perception was much more important than reality. We owed Ben for that one. But I consider us paid in full. We let him escape with $15,000, but not his dignity. That we had to take.

One of the recurring themes of my life is that you have to tiptoe the line between being respected and feared, and Ben illustrated that point perfectly—better than I ever could have myself.

A more practical positive to come out of the Ben fiasco was that William designed a "suspicious transaction report" as a safeguard. Further, we required that every bet taken on the computer be printed out and stamped on a time clock so that we had yet another guard against past-posting games. In addition to grading games by computer, we graded every single one of those bets by hand at night, just like we did in the "old school." And in a weird, nostalgic way, it warmed my heart that a con like Ben's got us back to doing business the way my dad always had. Old school, and by hand.

We gave Carlos a $1,000 bonus and word spread through the office that the only profit to be made in cheating us was by tipping us off to it.

Now that's good business.

13

A-Listers and Star Athletes: Welcome to Hollywood

AS OUR REPUTATION grew, we started to go mainstream. All of a sudden, A-list actors and professional athletes started to use our sports betting service. It was official: We had gone Hollywood.

Out of all of the A-listers we dealt with, the most entertaining were the pro athletes. In September 1997, I had a tout named Kevin Duffy who would send me a ton of whales. Kevin was Stu Feiner's top earner, and he was in charge of Stu's phone room. He was actually Stu's brother-in-law. They screwed each other so much that they stopped talking for a while, but that's the nature of being gorilla touts. Kevin used to tout all the big names and well-to-dos. The guy was so good that he could con oxygen out of water.

One day Duffy called me from New York with a "huge deal." He had an in with NHL hockey player Len Barrie of the Pittsburgh Penguins. Duffy had me on a three-way call to convince Barrie that we were completely legit and confidential and that he could bet large amounts with us with no problem. I warmed him up and reeled him in. I mean, let's face it: That's what I'd been doing since I was sixteen years old, so naturally I closed the deal.

Len wired $100,000 the very next day and started betting. He would bet $5,000 to $10,000 on football—we call that five to ten "dimes" a game. As we did with all VIP bettors, I sent Len on an all-expenses-paid trip to Vegas and got a spa suite for him and his girlfriend at the MGM. I saw this professional athlete as someone who could direct a lot of buddies to us, and the cost of that trip was pocket change compared to what he and his rich athlete friends were going to bet.

Obviously, Len had some big friends—and he sent them all to us—but none was bigger than the best player in the NHL at that time, Jaromir Jagr.

Jagr loved to bet football, and he loved calling in his bets right from the locker room. You could really tell that he got a huge kick out of calling in under his special code name, "975 JJ," and being involved in something a little dangerous. He would call us from the locker room right before his game started, betting hoops for the same night.

The most memorable Jagr bet occurred when his Penguins were at Madison Square Garden playing the Rangers one night. We always had his games on one of the TVs in the fish tank up over Eduardo's desk. Jagr was making his $40,000 bets right from the Garden locker room as his teammates were taking the ice. He could win or lose $250,000 in a week, so he was a whale. As soon as he heard his read-back and got his confirmation number, we turned to the TV to see him finally roll onto the ice, well after his teammates had already skated out.

One particular time, though, Jagr had a problem on the phone that took a lot more than a few minutes to resolve.

Jagr's credit card was maxed out, and he couldn't get any

action because we did not, under any circumstance, extend a credit line. We were a post-up business, period. That, of course, was one of the best aspects of running an offshore operation compared to running one on the streets in the U.S. We didn't have to extend ourselves by offering credit and hoping to get paid. All the money had to be posted up front before we would take a bet.

Many people might think I was a fool for not extending a multimillionaire like Jagr credit. But I'm no fool. Giving a high-profile guy like that credit is a recipe for disaster. If he ever owed me a bunch of money, he could tell me to get lost and then go bet elsewhere. If he never paid, what could I do? I wasn't in the streets and couldn't send someone to mess him up. Besides, he was the number-one player in the NHL—you don't send a tough guy to break his knees. On the other hand, even though we were a legal business in Costa Rica, I couldn't sue. Where would I sue—in the United States? Maybe I could sue in Fantasy Island court? It was a no brainer to never extend credit.

So after we respectfully told Jaromir that credit was not an option, he asked if we could do a three-way call with his bank. My general manager and 5 percent owner of the company at that time, Sandy Berger, got his bank on the speakerphone in my office.

This was a U.S. bank, and Jaromir proceeded to tell them in his broken English, "I'm Jaromir Jagr, my credit not enough. How can I live on such a small credit line?"

He told them he needed another $50,000 and needed it right now. They went back and forth for five minutes, and he got the extension. But before the banker hung up, Jaromir started talking to us.

"So, Sandy, can I bet now? Are all my bets good?" Jagr asked excitedly.

"Jaromir, Jaromir! I am still on the phone!" the banker yelled.

"Shut up! I need to know that my bets are in!" Jagr ordered.

Finally, I yelled back, "Your bets are good!" into the speakerphone while Sandy just stared at me in disbelief. We were on a three-way call accepting a bet from the best player in the NHL, with his U.S. bank on the line.

Jagr then repeated his account number on the phone, and he was set. We made all bettors repeat their account number to approve the read-back for a bet. This gave us a second chance to verify the account number before making the bet official. Like every other policy I had created, that is now a standard industry practice among all companies.

So after Jagr said his account number and hung up, the exhausted banker said, "Uh, gentlemen, I'm going to hang up now, okay?"

I told him that was fine. While it was an event the banker no doubt never forgot, for us it was another typical day at SDB Global. Jagr was a great customer, mostly because he couldn't pick his ass from his elbow. I don't remember him ever receiving a payment from us in all the time he played. He may have won a bet or two, but I am 100 percent certain he never had a winning week, ever. He might have been the biggest sucker I have ever dealt to in my entire career. He never met a favorite that he didn't just adore. It just goes to show you that nobody can win at betting sports, not even star athletes. The game is just not set up to breed winners.

One thing I want to make clear: We didn't let athletes bet on their own games or on their own sport. That would be wrong, not to mention illegal. Besides, we wanted to continue to fly under the radar—we weren't looking for scandals. If one of our bettor-athletes was nailed for betting on his own game or sport, it could have prompted an investigation by their league, and that would have led to us.

We didn't want the kind of attention that would have come with an athlete betting on his own sport. Now, don't get me wrong. Athletes wanted to bet on their own sport, even on their own teams at times, but we never let that happen. Athletes were the biggest sucker bettors of them all because they all thought they knew more about sports than the oddsmakers. In addition, they all had the kind of built-in, competitive nature that led them into always doubling down in an attempt to get even, which is a bad betting strategy. This made them really good clients. Like I said before, Jagr never had a winning week with us. Thank God he had a good day job—because he couldn't win a freaking bet to save his life.

I know that a lot of you are going to read this story and think that I am ratting these hockey players out to sell books. While I understand that position, it is not consistent with the truth. Here is how I feel about these hockey players betting on football and basketball: Who gives a flying puck? Why is it such a bad thing that an NHL player bet on a football game? Is it child pornography? No. Is it unethical? Immoral? Is it even newsworthy? No. Anyone who has ever filled out a bracket for NCAA March Madness in an office pool or who has ever bought even one lottery ticket has gambled. Why do you think there are fantasy leagues for baseball, football, basketball, hockey, and even auto racing? You pick a team and players after paying a franchise fee to be involved, and those whose players fare best win money. Cable networks air one-hour fantasy football programs on a weekly basis. Same thing for baseball. Pure and simple, these fantasy leagues are *gambling*—and also a lot of fun. The sports leagues themselves, the NFL, MLB, the NBA, and so on, don't say a word about the legality of these leagues and don't even comment about the fact that some of them use team and league logos in ads and on their websites. Why is that? Because these players are watching every game, reading every box score, following the games online, on TV, and on the radio, and are sports junkies because they have a personal stake in how the teams and players do. In other words, these are hard-core fans. Think the leagues want to lose these guys? These guys live and die with their teams and players. The leagues *need* these fans as sports compete for season tickets, advertising dollars, sponsorships, promotions, and viewerships.

Here is another thing: Without traditional sports gambling, there would be no leagues and the leagues know it. The leagues not only know that gamblers are their true TV audience but they protect the sanctity of the league for that very reason. The reason baseball got so upset at Pete Rose was not because he bet. It was because he bet on baseball, and that was akin to insider trading, which might have turned off the gamblers. The leagues make sure the gamblers feel confident in their product so that the gamblers will continue to bet and watch. Who do you think is watching an NFL game with two minutes to go and the home team ahead by thirty points? Only the people who bet the over/under, which will be determined by a potential score in the waning seconds, right? Of course I'm right. Why do you think that injury reports are kept on such tight lockdown? You are more likely to hear about a CIA leak than about an injury before it's officially reported. Why? Gambling. If someone knew about an injury before someone else, they would have an unfair advantage when gambling. So don't let anyone tell you that the leagues are anti-gambling, because it is quite the opposite. The sports leagues are built and structured with the gambler in mind.

• • •

WITHIN TWELVE SHORT months after setting up shop in Costa Rica, we had achieved global recognition beyond our wildest dreams. SDB Global was known as "the new way to bet sports, and bet big!" We had eighty-five clerks per shift taking bets from three thousand active clients per betting session. I had come a long way from peddling parlay cards at North Miami Beach High School, and no matter how you stacked it up, I was, by a large margin, what I had set out to be: the biggest bookmaker in the world.

Where else could you bet $100,000 on a game? Nowhere! Las Vegas would accept big bets on the Super Bowl, but we'd take $100,000 on any game that had a line. Where else could you win half a million bucks and get paid the next day with the kind of urgency and efficiency that made my name synonymous with the highest rollers in the world? Nowhere else. We would accept withdrawal requests twenty-four hours a day and have a check FedExed to the customer's door within forty-eight hours or we doubled the payment—that was our guarantee. That became our trademark: We pay, and we pay faster than anyone. It was the same motto that I had on the streets.

I finally started to realize that I had been carrying the reputation and the future of the entire offshore gaming industry on my back, and just as in Miami and Panama, I was operating with a philosophy and business practice that ultimately led to the complete validation of the industry. We paid everyone so fast that they quickly overcame their initial hesitation about sending their money overseas. Once that happened, customer deposit amounts quadrupled.

Guys who sent a few hundred to test us out would start sending thousands. We always passed the test because by this time

New York was so turned on by my results that they gave me their complete backing and the full strength to deal to the world. They backed me with unlimited bankroll, and that didn't include the millions in customer money on deposit that we were holding at all times. New York was the key. I showed Bo and Donnie the money, and they backed me to the nines. With unlimited bank behind me and an entire nation full of gamblers who needed a quality place to play, it was like shooting fish in a barrel.

I was getting players from everywhere—not just New York and Los Angeles but also Minnesota, Georgia, Texas, and Iowa. Yes, Iowa! You see, while there were a ton of gamblers in New York City and Philadelphia (which remain among the bookmaking capitals of the world), there were also lots of bookmakers in those cities who were willing to extend credit but would break your arms if you didn't pay. I didn't need to spend any money marketing in New York or Philly because I figured that they would all eventually find their way to me, broken arm in tow. So I spent my advertising money in towns where people had been dying to make a bet on a game but had no option other than a flight to Vegas. We marketed in Minnesota, Wisconsin, Colorado, Texas, etc. You think there were bookies in Wisconsin? Not a chance. Not real ones anyway. I liked being the only game in town. Why compete in towns that had local bookies when I could teach first-time suckers how to gamble instead? They had no choice but to think I was the best option because I was their only option. I felt like my dad in his infamous London card game hustle. Advertising in these cities was like putting in a cold deck. Game over!

In addition to running the operation, overlooking bookmaking, and supervising Sandy, William, and all my other executives, I also single-handedly controlled all marketing, PR, and anything creative that had to do with our company. This is why I always worked twelve- to fifteen-hour days, seven days a week, 363 days a year, only taking two days off in July for baseball's All-Star break. I was a workaholic and a control freak, and though I tried to hire a public relations and marketing firm at first, I just couldn't stomach paying them hundreds of thousands of dollars to negotiate media that I could negotiate myself. My marketing strategy kind of mirrored my life strategy in that I always picked my spot and then hit it with everything I had.

I knew right off the bat that my competition wasn't local bookies in the U.S., because there were only a limited number of states that even had bookies. My competition was actually Las Vegas, and calling me to make a sports bet would always be more appetizing than a flight to Vegas. Local bookies weren't my competition, because they gave credit and we never did. You can't get a credit customer who is getting paid on time from his local bookie to switch to posting up his money offshore. However, I was Moses to someone in the middle of Wisconsin, snowed in on a Sunday morning with nothing to do but watch football. This guy saw our ad, called our toll-free number, and was betting within fifteen minutes as he cooked a brat and drank a beer with his Packers cheese-head hat on! They loved us in the heartland, and we appreciated them, too.

I had novice bettors (a.k.a. suckers) coming in from all angles. We had eighty-five phones lit up, and after 11:30 on a Sunday we didn't take any bets less than $200! If you wanted to bet less than $200, you had to call before 11:30 AM on a Sunday, or before 10:30 AM on a Saturday (for college football). We were open twenty-four hours a day, and we opened up the betting line on Saturday night for the following Sunday's games, which gave customers more than a week to bet those games. Even so, many bettors still tried to place bets with one minute to go until kickoff. We had a bank of fifteen VIP phones that took no bets under $1,000. We had three phones in the war room (the fish tank) that took the real big bets, like $100,000 a game from the biggest customer in the world, code name "999 TV." His name was Karl Mowhawk, and he later got arrested in his home state of North Carolina for embezzling $50 million from his company to pay off his gambling debts. We took $50,000 a game from Jaromir Jagr and the hockey gang, $100,000 a game from the infamous Miami tout Adam Minor, and $100,000 a game from a Los Angeles betting agent who was supposedly a front man for several A-list actors.

One day a call came in from none other than Charlie Sheen. The secretaries didn't even realize who Charlie Sheen was, but I heard a page over the phone system that a "Charlie Sheen" was requesting to speak with a manager or an owner. I immediately had them direct the call to Sandy Berger, who I felt represented the best chance at closing, and I set up the call so that I could monitor it from my office. When Sandy got on the phone with Sheen, he immediately recognized Sheen's voice and knew that he was the real deal. I am sure Sandy was thinking the same thing as me: *Who better than Charlie Sheen to be our Hollywood poster boy?*

Sheen was a real gentleman on the call; he was genuinely excited about the product and about being able to bet over the phone. Sandy immediately opened an account for him and got all of his personal information. At that point I was thinking to myself, *This call is going great,* because nobody was better then Sandy at promoting the facts and making someone feel comfortable, but I was eager to close the fucking guy already and get his money. Just as I was thinking that, Sandy asked him the golden question in this process, "Mr. Sheen, do you have a pen?" This meant that Sandy was about to give him our wiring instructions, and we were in! I was thinking, *This is all but a done deal*. But just as I began counting the money, Sheen said to Sandy, "You need to call my Wilshire Boulevard office in Beverly Hills and speak to my controller girl to work out payment details." Sandy took the number and thanked him and assured him he would follow up immediately.

Being a bookmaker, I was always looking at situations and attaching odds to them. I had us a two-to-one favorite prior to the mention of controller girls and offices in Beverly Hills. After those speed bumps were laid, I had us as an even money (one-to-one) favorite. I knew from my experiences with these celebrity types that their controllers had their own ideas about where they wanted their clients' money to go. Therefore I knew this was no walk in the park. Whether or not we ever got the wire was irrelevant, because the fact that a guy like Charlie Sheen had heard about us, called us, and was impressed enough to open an account said so much about where we had taken the entire bookmaking industry. Do you think that guys like Charlie Sheen ever called my Brooklyn office back in the street bookmaking days of the early 1990s to open an account and bet? It would be a million-to-one shot. Now these types of things were becoming everyday occurrences. No question about it: As far as Hollywood and the A-listers were concerned, we had arrived.

It wasn't all stars and athletes though; we had the biggest touts and sports services on our payroll, and they earned good money from us for sending players. They operated at the street level, drumming up business for us on a daily basis via their own hundred-person call centers. It wasn't unusual to get twenty new ten-dime ($10,000) bettors in a week from touts like Stu Feiner Sports, Andy Karp and Brad Parker (Executive Sports in New York), Curtis (Colorado Sports), Lem Banker and Jim Hurley (from Baltimore), Wayne Root, Jimmy Spats, Bobby Delarocka (from Vegas), Adam Minor (from Miami), and many others.

Adam Minor was the best tout around—he controlled more whales than anyone in the business. He would operate in three different voices: a Chinese man, a Texan, and an Englishman. He would get people to bet every penny they had on a game with the utmost confidence that they had a sure thing. It was great for us, because where do you think all those big bets were placed? The only place that even took them, SDB Global. *Cha-ching!*

In the bookmaking business, music is when all the phones are ringing at once. I had the entire tout business on my payroll, and that kept the music playing all day long.

Nothing is easy. I had business coming at me from every angle, and while it took every ounce of me to keep it all running smoothly, I had to always be on top of infiltration from sharp bettors, otherwise known as wiseguys, or "sharpies." Wiseguys are sharp bettors, the professional gamblers who make up about 1 percent of the total gambling public. They beat the odds on a consistent basis and bury unknowing bookmakers all over the world. Guys like Billy Walters and splinter groups like the Kosher Kids and the Poker Players operate betting syndicates that are smarter than the Las Vegas oddsmakers who set the line for games.

So if you're wondering why I stayed business partners with my New York backers, Bo and Donnie, when I no longer needed the money, now you know. Nobody could ever sneak by them; they could spot wiseguys from a mile away. Luckily for me, my New York backers were not only my investors but professional sports bettors themselves, and part of the 1 percent who turned a profit betting on sports. They controlled a betting office in New York whose function was to make bets, not take bets. When they had a game going, they were getting hundreds of thousands down with twenty-five bookmakers. They were the sharpest betting syndicate on the East Coast, rivaled only by Billy Walters himself.

Needless to say, with their money on the line, they saw every ticket that came in over $5,000, and they scrutinized anything that looked odd. And they took action when needed.

It didn't happen often, but every now and then I would get a call on my cell phone from New York. They never called the office directly, only on my cell, and they would say, "Your customer number 230067. Get rid of him."

At that point, I would get the customer on the phone and personally tell him that we had identified him as an undesirable betting client and warn him not to try to come back. I would notify him that if he snuck back in, we would keep his money the next time. These bettors were actually humble about it, and all were grateful to get their money back in the first place. They were shills for professional betting outfits and weren't used to being treated with such dignity. Most of them respected me and did not return; when they did, we detected them and took their money.

Soon the word got out that we had zero tolerance for "sharp" or wiseguy business, and they stopped trying for the most part. We stayed on alert and made sure we kept out any professional bettors. This allowed me to treat everyone like a true retail customer. I could pay to have extra clerks on duty and go the extra mile for a client because we did such a good job of keeping the wiseguys and syndicate bettors as far away as possible. That is why the touts and sports services were the best sources for clients. Anyone who would listen to a salesman pitch him on a "guaranteed winner" certainly was our target schmuck.

I remember walking into the pits on most Sundays and allowing clerks on my regular lines to take bets under $1,000 till 1:15 PM, a good fifteen minutes after the games started. It didn't matter—do you think my clients had an advantage? They were novice bettors who were desperately trying to get their wagers in and enjoy some action. With three thousand bettors trying to get in to you at one time, you could have three hundred phone lines and it wouldn't be enough; some people would get busy signals, and that was just the way it was. That is why we adjusted the phone system so that we could handle the VIPs separately and ensure that they could always get an open line. But let's face it—if you wait until five minutes to game time to make your bet, you run the risk of getting screwed.

Nobody ever took bets until 1:15 PM before, but for me it was just more volume and more profit, a no-brainer on the books, and a special accommodation to the clients who were all suckers and couldn't win even if we let them bet in the second quarter. I was always trying to improve the overall experience. I knew how customers liked to be treated and what they deserved from their sports wagering service, and I gave it to them every single time they called.

Like I said, it was at that time that I started to realize the gravity of what we were doing. We had officially arrived at the next level. We were on our way to making many millions in our first year in Costa Rica, and we were changing the perception of the entire sports betting business. I was transforming sports betting from a stigmatized back-alley business into a futuristic stock brokerage company for sports bettors. Our customers used their credit cards and got their up-to-the-minute balance for their account on every call; the entire experience was far better than the classic bookmaking experience. We had become the preferred way to bet. Even customers who were used to getting credit with their local bookie were more than happy to leave those bookies when we gave them 10 percent bonuses for putting their money up and joining SDB Global. And all of a sudden customers we never targeted in towns like New York, Miami, Boston, and Philly started coming to us in droves. We were about to blow up the gambling world, and I knew it.

14

Unstoppable: A Gambler's Mind and a Bookmaker's Odds

BY THE START of the second year in Costa Rica, we were already up to two hundred incoming phone lines. I had bought the building next door and connected the two, separating our bookmaking and customer service departments completely.

We had turned into a ten-headed monster, and we needed every one of those heads to devour the business coming our way. We had five thousand unique bettors on Monday nights alone, making an average bet of $300. To put that in perspective, the average bet of an Internet sportsbook in today's marketplace is only $30; thus, our five thousand telephone clients were the equivalent of fifty thousand Internet clients today. We had a big fucking business, the biggest in the world. That is an important distinction, since every bookmaker you ever meet says he is the biggest in the world. Tell me something: Have you ever heard anyone claim they were the second- or third-largest bookmaker—or anything—in the world? No, everyone claims to be the biggest bookmaker in the world. It must be like a two-hundred-way tie for first place. Well, we were not numbers two or three. We were the biggest by all definitions of the word.

Our software and computer system could handle huge numbers and volume, so we ran like a well-oiled machine. This was all thanks to the tireless effort put forth by William to create an evolving system that would quickly bring one of the oldest manual professions out of the Stone Age and into the new modern world of technology.

About halfway through our second year, we were hearing a lot of talk from international bankers about valuations and the estimated worth of our company. Crunching the numbers, we were worth, conservatively, about $200 million. We received an informal offer from a representative for European bookmaker Victor Chandler of about half that. I could leave with a $100 million payday, or I could continue. Easy call. I was in it to win it, and I couldn't cash out with so many chips still out there to cuff.

Besides, between paying half to Bo and Donnie, and then kicking up half of what was left to you know who (my old man), that would have given me about $25 million to pay taxes on in the U.S., leaving me with about $15 million. Shit, $15 million would have seemed like a mountain of money to me back on the boardwalk in Atlantic City only three short years before this whole roller coaster began, when I was working for Caesar's as a glorified tour guide. But my eyes had gotten so wide from the experience that my entire scale of fortune had been thrown completely off. This was another recurring theme in my life: A little was always too much, and too much was never enough.

I had planned from the start in Costa Rica to go at least seven years before reevaluating and thinking about selling. I figured the people had spoken and unanimously elected me the King of All Bookies, a seat I had longed for since the day I booked my first parlay card slip from my high school gym teacher. Besides, I wasn't ready to give that seat up just yet. There were billions out there for the taking, and I'd be damned if I wasn't going to wait to properly cash in on what was rightfully mine.

WITH THE BUSINESS thriving, I wanted to make life in Costa Rica as fun and luxurious as I could. I upgraded houses and moved from a farmhouse on two acres in the hillside community of Santa Ana, just outside of San José, to a mountaintop mansion high in the hills of Escazu, the wealthiest suburb of San José. This wasn't a house, it was a small resort. Indoor and outdoor gardens stocked with fruit trees, three levels, five acres, and a *Lifestyles of the Rich and Famous*-style pool deck and entertainment area. I had ten maids, five butlers, two twenty-four-hour chauffeur/bodyguards, and a twenty-four-hour cook who provided room service. I had six bedrooms and a two-bedroom poolside guesthouse.

My wife liked Costa Rica but always missed Miami. It seemed like every time she came down she'd end up pregnant, and she felt more comfortable going through the pregnancies at home in Miami with both of our families around.

And to be honest, I was a young, successful gringo in the land of the walking papaya, and I enjoyed the time on my own in my completely pimped-out crib in the hills of Escazu, otherwise known as the City of Witches. I never got into more trouble than I could afford to. My wife would have thrown me out if I did. She was brutally tough, but so extremely sexy that I didn't give a fuck.

Besides, I just wanted her to be happy, and she was happy in Miami shopping at Bal Harbour and abusing my credit card far worse than any abuse I could have leveled onto some young Costa Rican hottie. The truth is, with me working twelve to fifteen hours a day, Costa Rica wasn't the best place for her to stay all year round, but she did love it in doses and fell in love with our help and all the people at work.

Everyone loved her, too. She was the quintessential boss's wife and the perfect complement to me, both personally and professionally. I had so much action at work, but she would get bored and miss home. She was genuinely excited that I was chasing a dream, and she understood that if I succeeded, it would set us up financially for the rest of our lives together, and for our children's lives, too. But she would still go stir-crazy after a few weeks in Costa Rica without even one department store—unless you consider Liz Claiborne a department store, and my wife didn't.

The parties we had when I was on my own in Costa Rica were unreal. We worked hard, but we played harder. We'd work fourteen hours a day and then party like we had ten hours left to live.

I was always comfortable with being the life of the party, an instinctive trait that I acquired working at Caesar's. In Costa Rica at the SDB mansion, I'd host the execs and management from our company for dinners and late-night insanity, though I never did mingle socially with the more than two hundred non-executive SDB employees. It was important, even with upper management, to keep that boss image intact and to never let my guard down with the same people I would have to give firm direction to the next morning.

Slowly but surely, I started to transition from tourist to native, not so much culturally but in the sense that my daily routine brought me satisfaction and had become my preferred state of being. Running the office gave me the opportunity to shine in my element. I was an authority on the art of bookmaking and bringing it to the masses. By this time I knew how it should look, sound, and be delivered to the end user. I had a gambler's mind and a bookmaker's odds behind me, and that made me feel unstoppable. Everything being done by the hundreds of employees in my space was inspired, engineered, created, and executed entirely by me.

My DNA was on everything in that office—especially the back-office secretaries, who were just beyond beautiful and tasted as sweet as they looked. While I often entertained the idea of moving back to the United States (it was popular among the Americans to sing the blues about being homesick), I realized that I was doing what I was born to do, doing it on a level higher than I had ever dreamed was possible, and Costa Rica was directly responsible for that. In fact, at this point I was raising the bar on a daily basis on what was thought to be the highest level.

I was very conscious of that throughout the ride, and very grateful, too. So while I was cocky, confident, tough, and strong, I was always grateful. I was grateful to my staff, grateful to my wife, and grateful to my creator. Looking back, that was probably the single quality that caused everyone to gravitate toward me and always rally behind me. I was a great leader because I was grateful for the opportunity to lead. You cannot lead if you are not strong, steady, and willing to get your hands dirty each and every day. You also cannot be a successful leader if you are not a grateful one.

I was in love with Costa Rica and my business. While things were going great, the level of our success and the stratospheric growth of the company worried me. Whenever I was putting out a fire, I was focused on the task at hand, so I didn't have time to be concerned about the evils that lurked. But when things ran smoothly, I'd have time to worry. Fueled by the high stress and pressure, those three and a half years in Panama and Costa Rica were like an emergency room—working long days, seven days a week. I had people trying to steal from me, mob guys trying to take a piece of me, and competitors trying to copy or wreck me. And I was trying to always stay gray, one step ahead of the FBI. I never was able to shake that concern and take a rest during the entire ride. I may have slept every night, but I never really rested.

AFTER A YEAR and a half had passed, I was everything but a statesman in Costa Rica. (I'd later be offered citizenship.) Not only did I bring more than three hundred jobs to the country (and legitimize the industry to gamblers worldwide), but I put Costa Rica on the radar screen for international commerce, period. The next thing we knew, several midsize bookmaking companies had popped up, and that meant more well-paying jobs for the deserving Costa Ricans.

Costa Rica is a country of educated people who are more than able to accomplish the task at hand and more than willing to play ball, at all levels. This was such a sharp contrast to the rape-and-pillage mentality of the lingering dictatorship we encountered in Panama.

The mayor of San José got a package from us each month. He played ball. Everyone saw the potential of what we were doing, and they all played ball with us and overlooked the fact that we were operating in a gray area not clearly defined by U.S. law, at least not as of yet. Costa Rica even let us advertise that we were licensed by the government, even though there weren't any licenses for sports gambling in Costa Rica then. Ironically, there aren't any now, either. Every single sportsbook that claims to be licensed in Costa Rica is doing so predicated on a scenario that I laid out in the San José mayor's office.

And here is how that unfolded: I received a call from the mayor's office one day asking me to come downtown right away for a meeting. My first call was to Alberto Moke to check whether his monthly envelope had been delivered. It was, so this summons really concerned me. I called Sandy and asked him to accompany me just in case I needed his advanced Spanish-speaking skills to gain a slight advantage from the warm and fuzzy feeling that Latinos get from speaking in their native tongue. Sandy was able to leverage his fluency for all it was worth, putting a great face and mouthpiece on our local political front. So we jumped in a car with a driver and headed down to the mayor's office; we smoked three joints on the way, downed a bottle of mouthwash, and hit the meeting running. Understand this: I could smoke ten joints and always hit a meeting fresh and ready to knock 'em dead. That's just a Stevo thing.

Upon arrival, we were greeted in typical Costa Rican fashion: How's your family? How's your company? How's your dog? How's your house coming along? And that was just the doorman. By the time we got past the secretaries and into the mayor's office, it was forty-five minutes later and we'd been greeted by dozens and assured them all of the well-being of everyone we knew.

Once we finally got into the mayor's office, we met, as usual, with a special representative. All of these meetings were always done via a rep, never with the mayor himself.

So we were sitting in a conference room with Miguel, the representative of the San José mayor, and he was visibly upset. I wasn't too worried because—let's be honest—that package we gave the mayor each month was enough money to send his entire family to school, an Ivy League school. We needed each other; I knew that, so I figured that he probably knew that, too.

Miguel said the mayor had been reviewing our brochure and noticed that it said we were "government-licensed." "Costa Rica does not have government licenses for betting sports. Why did you put that in there?" Miguel asked Sandy, in Spanish. Sandy turned to me and explained that this was about us saying that we were licensed.

I jumped up and responded to Sandy in English. "This is what the mayor wants to know?" I asked. "This is why he dragged us down here?"

That prompted Miguel to say, in perfect English, "It was not the mayor who asked you here, it was me. It is my job to foresee future problems and eliminate them. Now I ask you again: Why would you say you were licensed when we don't officially offer sports gambling licenses?"

I was pissed off. Offended.

"Show me where my literature says that we have a sports gambling license!" I demanded, thumbing through the brochure. "It doesn't!"

I finally found the page he was referring to and held it up.

"It just says, 'SDB Global is licensed by the government of Costa Rica.' And we are!" I said, raising my voice. "In my office I have a business license, issued to me by the Minister of Business and Employment. It is that license that I was referring to in my literature. I do have a business here, in good standing with all ministries, which employs two-hundred-plus employees at wages 35 percent higher than the national average for similar job descriptions. Do you deny that? This is not false advertising. We are licensed to operate a business in Costa Rica, a business that is not disallowed by Costa Rican law."

The irony was that not only were we operating in a gray area of U.S. law, but because there was no law against or allowing bookmaking in Costa Rica, we were operating in a gray area of Costa Rican law, too.

Miguel grew quiet, clearly shocked by how boldly I was willing to state the facts and defend my position. So I continued in a more modest, humble tone.

"Now, don't get me wrong, I am not saying that we don't get a benefit by the inference that we have a license specific to sports gambling, and I am also not saying that it wasn't by design," I said. "What I am saying is that we are all a team. Going forward, I'd like to start getting the benefit of the doubt on these issues. I shouldn't have to rush from my office down here because of something so minor. I respect that you want to do a good job, but please leave us to do ours."

Miguel stormed out of the room, leaving Sandy and me to sit and contemplate what was going on. Sandy was very concerned that I might have overstated our position. Fifteen minutes passed before the mayor himself walked into the room with his bodyguard. This was our first face-to-face.

"Which one is Steve Budin?" he asked in a strong voice.

"I am," I said, extending my hand.

"Thank you for choosing Costa Rica for your business," he said.

He shook my hand and left the building as fast as he had emerged. It was quick, but it was significant. I winked at Sandy as I watched the mayor exit.

ANOTHER DAY I got a call from Sandy, who had been on the phone with our lawyer, Jorge de la Guardia, directly connected to Costa Rica's president. Sandy had some bad news, which I had expected because things were just going too well. The fact that he had walked all the way from the other side of our building rather than just call me told me it was serious. Sandy walked in like he had just witnessed a murder.

"Ayyyyy, who fucking died?" I asked.

"I just got off the phone with our political envoy, de la Guardia," Sandy said. "The Costa Rican equivalent of the IRS has raised an issue regarding sports betting as it pertains to Costa Rican tax law. The only betting tax law on the books in Costa Rica is for the lottery. So for us . . ."

Because there was no other tax law, the Costa Rican government's argument was that it applied to all gambling. It was a nearly 75 percent tax and could close us down. I instructed Sandy to meet with our legal team and liaisons to the Costa Rican president to find out if there was a way out of this. If there was not, we'd need to stall and prepare to head for Antigua. That thought didn't appeal to me, and I hoped to hell the Costa Rican government would think about the big picture on this and realize what the loss of one thousand high-paying jobs from all the sportsbooks would do to its economy. And lest they doubted my resolve, I had moved the business successfully once, and I could do it again.

This possible obstacle really haunted me. I had put in almost two years, and I couldn't just take us to another country and start again. I didn't want to be caught in a constant cycle of rebuilding. I didn't sleep that night. I smoked fifty-three joints and drank twenty-five cups of Earl Gray tea in my backyard.

And then it hit me.

At 3:30 AM, I called an emergency meeting at my house, waking up Sandy, William, and Percy and getting them to come over. Our very existence was being threatened, so this just couldn't wait until 9 AM.

The guys showed up and were shaken and nervous about the situation. I knew that business was business, whether it was on the streets of New York or in the comparatively safe havens of corporate Costa Rica. Shit is going to always hit the fan, so you had to either turn the fucking fan off or at least redirect it away from you.

"We endured far worse shit in Panama," I told them. "It always seems like we are doomed, and we always find a way. This will be no different."

Sandy was on edge. He had the legal mind, and he saw no loopholes.

"What are we going to do, Stevo? Move to Antigua now? We're like a freaking carnival, a traveling bunch of bookmaking freaks," he snapped.

I loved Sandy, but that pissed me off. I wanted to rip his head off, but I needed to be calm because everyone was watching, and the last thing my top execs needed was me freaking out.

"What if we booked the bets in Antigua, but never had to set foot there?" I asked. They looked puzzled—they saw something starting to form, but couldn't yet make sense of it.

"Yeah," Sandy said with a hint of optimism. "Keep going."

"What if we simply changed ourselves from a gambling company to a technology company in Costa Rica that processes information for a gambling company in a country outside of Costa Rica—and more importantly, a company not subject to Costa Rican tax law? Antigua, Bahamas, Saint Kitts, wherever you want. We get a fee of $200,000 a year plus expenses to run the operation for the actual betting company, which we locate outside the country. Therefore, our taxes would be only on the

$200,000 service fee. This would be win-win for Costa Rica, our employees, and us. Yeah, we eat $145,000 in taxes, which is huge to this government, but we can stay in this country that I love for a very small token."

Sandy stood up and shrieked, "But the bets would still be taken in Costa Rica, no?"

I turned to William and said, "What if the bets were taken on a server outside the country and simply *processed* in Costa Rica? Then it would simply be data entry, not bet processing. Are you getting my drift here, guys?"

"I fucking love it!" Sandy yelled. "Stevo, this is fucking great!" He gave me a high five like we were back on the basketball courts of south Florida where we originally met.

I then turned back to William and Percy.

"Is it feasible?" I asked them.

William looked at Percy, who thought about it for a moment.

"How many weeks do we have?" Percy asked.

"We don't have weeks," Sandy snapped once again. "There's a delegation from the Costa Rican minister of taxes coming over. We have days, not weeks."

"No way," Percy said. "It's not doable."

They were not thinking about how it could be done but instead about what stood in our way. It's a common mistake among upper management. Hell, I couldn't figure it out in tangible terms, but I knew that my idea was our way out and that it would work.

Then it hit me. "Wait just a fucking minute," I said, more firmly than I probably needed to. "I didn't ask if it was doable. I asked if it was feasible. In other words, can it be done in theory? Can a server be set up in another country, a betting server? Can we process the information and transfer it to the betting server outside of Costa Rica for the actual booking of the bet, then receive a confirmation number back and give that to the customer? What I want to know is if that is technically feasible."

Percy caught on to what I was saying.

"Okay, yes, yes, absolutely, it is certainly possible to set up a system that accomplishes that," Percy said. "However, it might take a month."

They were still missing my point. Playing cards is sometimes about bluffs, and we had to bluff the Costa Rican government to beat them at this high-stakes game of poker they had engaged us in—for their benefit as well as ours. Let's face it: They were rooting for us to win and didn't want to be the government that lost what was almost one thousand jobs by that point, factoring in all of the sportsbooks operating in Costa Rica at that time.

"Guys, do you really think that the Costa Rican government is going to fly to the other country and check to see if we have a server there?" I asked the group. "Do you think they want to pay for flights and hotels, deal with a government that is competing for business with them, and ask to see the servers? No freaking way!"

The pieces had clicked for William. He was so excited that he started speaking fast, almost out of control.

"I get it, Stevo," William said, tripping over the words he couldn't get out fast enough. "You're saying to fake it . . . that is pure genius!"

The little light went on above Sandy's head. Drifting behind the power curve, he was now up to speed.

"I fucking love it," Sandy said for the fourth time in less than four minutes.

Percy, who still hadn't caught on, interrupted.

"What do you mean, 'fake it'?" Percy asked.

William, who by that point had become almost equal to Sandy in the company hierarchy, in theory if not in practice, explained.

"Look, what if I design a program tomorrow that makes it so every time a bet is taken by a clerk and submitted to the system, the screen shakes and a box comes up that reads, say, '*Connecting* to Bahamas, *sending* bet, bet *approved* in Bahamas,' and then a confirmation screen pops up? You see, that would be exactly what it would be like if it were actually happening."

Sandy was on board.

"I fucking love it," he said again. This was five times if you are keeping score at home. Sandy had been to Antigua back when I was looking for a place for us to escape to from Panama. So he knew what a shithole Antigua would have been to live in for us, and he wanted to stay in Costa Rica at any cost.

"Anything to keep us in Costa Rica," Sandy said. "I fucking love it." That was six.

I was smiling by then. Adrenaline was rushing through me, balancing out the THC from all the weed I had smoked and the caffeine from all the tea I had consumed. Aside from having to take a piss that would have filled the pool we were sitting by, I was on cloud nine.

Sandy stood up from his perch atop a lounge chair and asked us one last time.

"So whoever is watching this take place would have no choice but to believe it was happening, whether it was our clerks or the Costa Rican government's tax squad, right?" Sandy asked.

"That's correct," Percy shot back.

"I fucking love it!" Sandy exclaimed for the seventh and final time.

Percy was now fully on board and started thinking out loud.

"I can attach a cable, a red cable, between the server and the Telemux—something extremely visible that I will explain accommodates the transfer of data between the servers," Percy said, talking himself and us through it and smiling at his own role in moving my plan closer to reality.

Three days later, we found out that the team that would come to verify our claim would be headed up by a man named Alejandro—an ex-student of William's assistant programmer, Franco, who had been a professor at Costa Rica's best university. On top of that, Alejandro used to work for Percy at the ICE, the Costa Rican phone company, before I hired Percy away from them.

So we felt a lot better about pulling it off, because Alejandro would not be able to argue with his ex-boss and former professor. My first thought after the poolside council, and after talking to my father in Miami, was to reach out to this Alejandro guy and stick either a bundle of cash in his pocket or a gun in his ear. My dad was still my top adviser, even though by this time he was completely out of the loop. He thought I should talk to William and Franco and get their two cents before I started threatening anyone or stuffing their pockets with cash.

William and Franco were able to convince me to not bribe or threaten Alejandro. They said he was a man of integrity and wouldn't go for that. They told me to let them handle it. I respected their opinion, though it was against my better judgment. You have to know when to go with your hired guns, even when you disagree. But what is the sense of surrounding yourself with insiders and intellectually advanced people if you can't take their direction and use it to your advantage?

So I considered playing it straight and letting William, Percy, and Franco deliver. Little did they know that, once again, the fate of the entire industry (present and future) was hanging in the balance.

They were magnificent! It was 100 percent Hollywood, just a perfect production.

William hooked up the program just as he had explained. Percy connected the red wire from the server to the phone system. The delegation came in on a slow day, but we had every employee there and in uniform. Before William and Percy showed the group the technical routine, I personally took them on a tour around the office for an hour, stopping at key employees' desks and letting the team members talk to them about what they did and what they thought of the company.

I also allowed them to wander around the huge facility and talk to employees without us watching. Although this was not part of their planned visit to our office, I wanted to personalize the situation. By the time they were ready to see William and Percy's show, they were completely aware of the gravity of the decision they were about to make and what it would mean to all the local people they'd just met, people whose jobs with SDB Global had changed their lives.

The Percy and William show took four minutes. Alejandro seemed to buy it hook, line, and sinker, too. He shook their hands, congratulated them, and wished them well. On the way out, William saw Alberto Moke, my chief local negotiator, hand Alejandro a manila envelope that seemed to be stuffed pretty thick.

William turned to me with a shocked look on his face.

"I thought you were going to leave it to me?" William said.

I looked at him and smiled for a few seconds.

"William," I said, "I didn't get to where I am today by leaving things to other people. It's just not my style."

William just laughed. It was obviously party time, as we had dodged another bullet. But you couldn't help but wonder how long we could keep dodging bullets until we eventually took one between the eyes.

The irony is that to this day every sportsbook operating out of Costa Rica (and there are now more than one thousand of them) is faking it and claiming the same thing—that they are not taking the bets in Costa Rica but simply processing the information for betting companies outside of Costa Rica.

Imagine that.

This story, unfortunately, is not without tragedy.

Sadly, we lost Percy two days later. We partied for two days straight, and Percy, who could drink Dean Martin under a table, lost control of his car late Saturday night, hit a tree, and was killed. It was a terrible event that shocked us all. We loved Percy. He was a major part of our evolution. Percy was a loner and never had a girlfriend. Instead, he was married to technology, a real tech geek, a Napoleon Dynamite. But he was a genius, and I still miss him.

That was very typical of the entire ride we were on: highs of epic proportions and lows that seemed to pin us in with no escape. And the higher the highs were, the bigger the drop around the next bend always seemed to be.

The ecstasy of beating the Costa Rican government's probe took us up to the top again, but losing Percy brought us all down for quite a while. I thought about my family, and how much I missed them.

There was only one more mountain to climb, Internet Peak, where the final pot of gold at the end of the rainbow was. After that, I thought, I'd reevaluate. Maybe even sell the business and cash out for good.

If only I'd had a crystal ball.

15

Dot-com Dollar Signs

I **MET SANDY AND** William for our usual 6:00 PM pot-smoking session in back of my private office each day. This was important because it gave the three of us great bonding time and a chance for me to bounce my ideas off the two smartest guys in the company, both of whom were the antithesis of yes-men.

William and Sandy had a little bit of competition going, vying for my recognition and that top spot in the company under me. I used to let William get away with murder, which really bothered Sandy.

Sandy understood deep down why I always gave William the benefit of the doubt: He was so valuable, a great kid, and his knowledge of technology—and how to write software programs—was driving our operation forward. That being said, I gave Sandy 5 percent of the company and William only 1 percent, so it should have been obvious where I stood. We made $20 million gross in our last year, so those percentages translated into big dollars.

So we were smoking a joint, a good one. We used to smoke this stuff that Felix from customer service (whose job it was to get us good shit) called Cajeta. It was named after a popular Costa Rican hard chewy candy made of sugar and milk called *cajetas*.

I looked at Sandy and said, "We are going to be bigger than the casinos on the Vegas Strip one day."

Sandy, who loved to play devil's advocate, replied, "Slot machines and blackjack will always be more profitable than sports, Stevo. So how are you going to manage that?"

The plan had already formed in my head.

"Look, guys, while the touts and Scorephone advertising have built this business into a monster beyond all of our original expectations, the single biggest growth area in our business has been Internet advertising," I explained. "The Internet is changing the way the world does business. There is a new breed of person being created out there who wants the Internet experience, even though it is not as easy as picking up the phone and telling us what they want directly. They are loyal to the Internet, and the more we can give them to do on the Internet, the more they will be loyal to us."

William was right on my wavelength and jumped right in.

"Stevo is right," William said. "Right now, our Internet page is only a business card to the world, and while it is very effective in getting the phone to ring, are we really using it to its full potential?"

I got right back in, as I wanted to personally drive home the point. I stood up on an exposed pipe that was about three feet off the ground and started to preach the gambling gospel according to me.

"Why just give out the info and a toll-free number?" I asked. "Why not actually open the accounts online? Give our lines out online so we don't have so much phone traffic from line shoppers. Maybe offer some contests and games."

Sandy jumped in, always ready to argue. Remember, he has a criminal defense lawyer background and can argue any side of any issue effectively. And he was always more than willing to engage.

"Live lines are a great idea. Opening accounts online is good too," Sandy said. "But I don't see how free Internet contests and games are going to increase sportsbook revenue."

I jumped down from the pipe and looked at everyone, knowing I had a rocket in my pocket and I was about to launch it. "What if those games and contests were actually video slots, blackjack, and poker for real money?" I asked. "What if we didn't just open accounts online but took deposits and took bets online? Casino bets and sports bets! Even if it's a pain in the ass, it's the future. We can lead or we can follow, but Internet gambling is the future. In fact, I declare to you right fucking now that phone betting as we know it is all but a dead man walking once the Internet takes over as the main communication device and transactional device for business."

Sandy stayed his combative course.

"You want to take a bet for 10K from a guy over the Internet, with no tape and no proof. What bettor is going to do that?" he asked.

William the computer genius was already running software ideas in his head.

"Stevo, I've never done transactional Internet programs, but I think what you are saying in concept absolutely works," William said. "You just make the customers into the clerks and give them a watered-down version of the clerk screen."

I put my hand on Sandy's shoulder as if to tell him it was time to get on the train.

"I don't expect a $10,000 player to ever bet online, and we

16

Playing the Final Hand You're Dealt

AS YOU'LL RECALL from the opening chapter, we never did make it online with bet taking. I had that deal with CBS's SportslineUSA.com on the table and had to walk away from Jackson Harris and a billion dollars. My father was arrested in Miami, and it was time to call it a day. It felt like getting off the roller coaster at the top with the highest, most exciting plunge right in front of you.

After being forced to surrender to the FBI and endure the process of being processed, I returned to Miami and waited for my court case to be resolved. I was really feeling down at the time, and upset. I felt like online and offshore gambling was my baby, and I now had to watch everyone have their way with her. Did my arrest stop the industry I had created? Hell, no. It simply sent thirty thousand active bettors looking for a new place to play. Twenty-five new companies opened the very same week that we were forced to close by the U.S. government.

It became obvious to me at the very beginning of my case that the U.S. government would not be going after any other companies. The investigative costs coupled with the types of fines and sentences they got in return simply did not add up or justify prosecution from a dollars-and-cents perspective. Like a lot of things, it was just a media event—some good PR to justify asking for more funds and hiring more agents to keep the world safe from Internet betting.

I was getting screwed because I was the big fish and the token sacrificial lamb. This was the prize I was getting for being the best at what I did. I was forced to watch from the sidelines as everyone gobbled up my clients and the industry I had pioneered along with them.

I knew what I'd lost here. I knew the dollar amount, and it was a billion-dollar figure. It was a disaster. By this time, www.Sportsbook.com, the URL I was supposed to buy right before I got pinched, was making about $4 million a month and starting to pull away from the pack. I just felt like this was all so unfair.

I was at rock bottom, emotionally and spiritually.

I was petitioning God from under the big oak tree in my backyard in Miami, just pacing in thought and prayer. "What did you do to me?" I asked. "Why did it all have to end this way?" I strongly believe in God and karma and believe that everything happens for a reason. "What did I do to deserve this?" I asked. "I'm a good person overall, not without fault and a few slips, but compared to what was going on around me in Panama and Costa Rica, I was a freakin' saint! Why, God? Why me?"

What I realized was that when you ask God a question, it's not always answered in the way it is asked or in the time frame you would like. In addition, you don't always get the answer you want to hear.

Several months had passed, and I was at the end of my pretrial court arrangement. I remember that I couldn't wait to be done with the probation-style monitoring that I was under. Besides, I couldn't wait to smoke a joint already. I had to drop piss for these guys once a week because when they originally booked me, my piss was dirtier than the Chi-Cha juice sold by street vendors in Panama.

I was sitting in the backyard of my newly built, Miami Beach estate, staring at my reflection in the resort-style pool I had just installed. I noticed that the image staring back at me was young, energetic, and way too handsome to be filled with all this animosity and "woe is me" tone.

I picked my head up and looked all around my backyard. I saw that my two beautiful daughters, Jackie and Juliette, were running around laughing and playing. My gorgeous wife Melisse was watching over them. Like a rock, she was unfazed and unblemished by the entire ordeal. Unlike everyone else, she wasn't worried about our future. She believed in me. And it dawned on me that the only one who was mourning there was me.

I suddenly realized that to be bitter and resentful in the face of such enormous blessings was a sin. I realized that God had blessed me with a family whose love was worth far more than the hundreds of millions of dollars of profit that my bookmaking business had stood to bring me in the coming year alone. This family that I had all but ignored for the past four years while I played CEO and built an empire from scratch was God's gift, and it was right in front of me—to be the husband and father I always wanted to be was finally within my reach.

I had been willing to sacrifice everything to achieve my financial goals, and I almost lost what was most precious to me without ever realizing its true value. I had certainly lost touch with my priorities. I had placed the entire family on cruise control while I poured every emotion I had into the business.

I found myself on my knees in my backyard crying and thanking God. It had been so long since I thanked God for anything. I had spent the last four months cursing God and everyone else—blaming them for what I was certain was the worst event that would ever happen to me. I thought I would never recover. It's funny how a little divine perspective can change you from the inside out. It makes you grateful in the face of what appears at first to be tragedy. If you are always focused on the negative aspects of your life, you get no value whatsoever out of the positive.

I had been drifting further and further away from my family as the demands of work became greater and greater. As the numbers grew and grew, so did the partying and the type of behavior that wasn't conducive to being a family man. Don't get me wrong: everyone in my family was taken care of and they lived the lifestyle of the rich and famous, but my heart and soul was elsewhere. To get that billion, I would have done anything, and that was just wrong.

For the first time, I realized that there was nothing more important than family. There was no amount of money that was worth more than my family. I picked my crying ass up off the ground and rededicated myself to the things in life that were really important. I recommitted myself to being a father and a husband. I promised God and myself that I would never again lose focus on what was most important. I swore that I would never forget the value of my wife Melisse and my two angels, Jackie and Juliette.

This change in my mentality was sudden and instantaneous. I was a changed man in a matter of minutes. I had been pissed off for four months straight, without a single good day, and then the light went off and I finally got it. I received God's answer to my question: Why *me?* His answer was: Because you are blessed.

I went inside the house a new man. I had my swagger back, my smile back, and, most importantly, my spirit was back. My dad, who was visiting us at the time, was sitting on the couch.

"You know, Dad, I think it's time to move on and do something new," I said.

My father doesn't talk a lot about religion, but on this day he was in that frame of mind and offered some great perspective.

"Son, when somebody dies, according to the Jewish religion, you sit shivah. You sit for seven days. God mandates seven days for you to mourn and pay respects," he said. "It's not so much to make you cry, necessarily; you do that on your own. It's to say that on day number eight you must get up, go on with your life, and pursue happiness. That's what we're here for, Steven. You moan, you cry, you even bitch, but then you must go on with your life. Losing your business is really no different than losing a loved one."

He was 100 percent correct. Part of my life had come to an end, but if I dealt with it properly, it could be the start of something entirely new, and it certainly was.

As the current CEO of the biggest conglomerate of sports handicapping websites in the world, I have once again revolutionized an industry and successfully taken the sports gambling picks business from the gutter to the corporate level. My websites SportsAdvisors.com and WhoWillCover.com are the largest handicapping sites on the Web. The only site that brings in more revenue is BrandonLang.com, and I own and operate that, too.

That site features Brandon Lang, who, as previously mentioned, was immortalized in the movie *Two for the Money*, starring Al Pacino and Matthew McConaughey. *Two for the Money* accurately depicts the state of the sports handicapping business prior to my takeover. It was a shady business that preyed on greedy suckers who thought they could buy their way to success at gambling. It was a pure scam. Not anymore.

All of my pick sites sell picks and analysis to gamblers across the country at a fair price. No hype, no scam, no thievery. Gamblers don't bet with me anymore, but they buy their picks and analysis from me now. With customers in the tens of thousands, I am once again changing the way the world gambles. I successfully took the tout business out of the hands of the scumbag hustlers operating their phone rooms and sucking thousands out of each pitiful sucker, and I replaced their cons, lies, and cold calls with credible analysis over the Internet from credible handicappers. With gross sales from my handicapping sites reaching the $10 million mark last year, it's obvious that the people out there love the new direction I have introduced. I now have over ten sites that dominate the Internet landscape.

If you are buying a pick online from a credible website, chances are you are paying me, and that is a good thing for you. While I can't guarantee that we will make you into an instant winner, I can assure you that the pick and analysis you buy from me will be well worth the $24 you pay for it and that it will certainly increase your chances of winning more or losing less over the long run. That is in stark contrast to the animals I took this industry over from. These guys would call a customer over the phone, insist that they had bought a referee, and then get the customer to pay $5,000 or $50,000 for a sure thing. There is no such thing as a sure thing, but because some suckers are greedy enough to believe the lies, they sent their money. Not anymore. Under my guidance and direction, the online hand-icapping business is slowly climbing out of the gutter and starting to be considered credible, in much the same way the bookmaking business became credible offshore while it was under my control.

My current successes don't stop there. Most recently, I've opened yet another "lifestyle and entertainment" company called NakedPapers.com. Naked Papers sells clear rolling paper made from cellulose. Look, there only a few things that I am an expert in. Gambling and smoking are certainly two of them. So isn't it fitting that I would wind up owning a rolling-paper company?

While vacationing in Brazil in late 2006, I was introduced to the concept by a local shaman-pharmacist who handed me two sheets of what looked like plastic and told me to try smoking out of them for the best smoking experience of my life. He then explained that the main ingredient in the clear paper was cel-lulose, which is extracted from a eucalyptus plant in gel form and dried on trays. Needless to say, he didn't have to twist my arm to get me to try. I tried it that night in my hotel and was hooked. I loved it. It had no taste, no smell, and no glue or harmful chemicals, but most of all it was so cool. As you know, I believe everything happens for a reason. I went to the local Brazilian company that manufactured this cellulose paper and cut a deal that ultimately led to the birth of Naked Papers Inc.

Just like I guessed could happen the very first time I tried it, Naked Papers is now the hottest smoking accessory in the United States. In successfully bringing this product to the masses, I have proven to myself that I can do anything I put my mind to as long as I am passionate about it.

At the end of the day, I am a visionary who is simply not satisfied with money alone. I like to put my signature on a product and forever change the way the world does things. I changed the way the world gambles by going offshore in 1994 and pioneering what is now the multibillion-dollar online gaming industry. I changed the way those same gamblers buy their picks and get their scores, odds, and relevant gambling information when I took over the sports handicapping industry in March 2003. And now I am going to change the way the world smokes. So when you're walking down the street in the West Village of New York City and see a bunch of hippie-like socialites smoking something wrapped in a Naked Papers rolling paper, remember—I told you so!

The bottom line is this. Where it used to take every ounce of my energy to operate one business, SDB Global, I am now running over fifteen separate businesses and exceeding expectations for all of them. This is something I could have never done in my twenties. However, it is directly because of my experiences in my twenties—the ups and, more importantly, the downs—that I am able to handle whatever is thrown at me. What this means, my friends, is that the game is always won in the fourth quarter. No matter how bad things look at any time, keep in mind the stage of the game you are in, and save a rally for the end.

I am happy to report that, as it stands now, I am on top of my game and fully engaged in chasing my dreams again. Only this time I haven't lost my focus on what is most important. I know that I owe everything to my wife and kids, and I will never forget that again. No matter how demanding my current schedule is, I never miss a day to be carpool dad. I am home every night for dinner, and I never let my wife forget that I am crazy about her in every way. She is, and always was, the glue.

God's answer to me was that what I thought was a curse was

actually my biggest blessing in disguise. This fully hit home on December 4, 2002, with the birth of my one and only son, Jace David Budin. I picked him up in my arms and kissed his precious face. I handed him back to my glowing wife and kissed her on her forehead. My father was first in the door, and when he saw little Jace in my wife's arms, he couldn't help but tear up. He grabbed me and embraced me for the first time in four years. The last time we embraced like that we were standing in a cold New York jail cell having lost it all.

Four short years later, we had come full circle. Again.

Without even saying it, I could feel his message to me through his embrace. For the first time I could start to understand his feelings for me. Now that I had a son of my own, I could understand his fears, his rage, his intensity. Now that I had a son, I could start to understand the depth of his love, and the overwhelming pressure that fathering a son brings. I know that I have to complete the circle, and it is no doubt the toughest challenge I have ever faced to date. My father has been the driving force behind my every success.

He is my friend, my teacher, and my hero, and I would have my work cut out for me to try to follow in his footsteps. As we stood there in the hospital room celebrating the birth of my son, I knew that I would now have to be there for my son in the same way that my dad had always been there for me. I knew that once again my father was passing me the torch, and it was now my turn to step to the plate and face the music.

I knew that had I never been stopped in Costa Rica and arrested, I'd never have been celebrating Jace's first birthday four years later. I was the luckiest man on earth that day, and I owed it all to those freakin' FBI agents who busted me.

Every job, every relationship, every story—and every life—

has an arc with a beginning, middle, and end point. I thought my wild ride had a few more miles left on it. But it stopped when it needed to stop, and I was able to get off it just in time to start the rest of my life—the really important part.

Glossary

BOOKMAKING TERMS

My bookmaking career started in the streets of New York and Miami and ended up in the jungles of Central America. In that ten-year span, I was immersed in the language of the streets, especially bookie terminology. Bookmakers have their own words for everything. That is partly because you always want to talk in code when you operate an illegal business, and partly because it's just so damn cool! Here is an A to Z of all the relevant words we used as bookmakers. It is a great mix of the basics and real inside industry terms.

ACROSS THE BOARD: Betting on a horse to win, place, and show (meaning to come in first, second, or third).

ACTION: (1) Placing a bet on a baseball game without stipulating a pitcher. (2) A gambler's pending bets. A gambler refers to his bet on a game as "action" on a game.

ACTION POINTS: A sophisticated bet in which the bettor is paid extra for every additional point his team covers the point spread by—or is charged extra for every additional point his team doesn't cover by. This type of bet can be done only in football and baseball for complete games.

ATS: Against The Spread. Used when discussing stats ("That team is five-and-one ATS").

BAD BEAT: A tough loss usually caused by a last-second unforeseen event.

BAGMAN: An intermediary who picks up and delivers money. A collector.

BANKROLL: The financial backer of a gambling operation (also called BR).

BEARD: A front man. Usually a proxy bettor, but can also refer to a figurehead or a fake owner who takes any heat in place of the real owner.

BETTING CARDS: A betting system in which gamblers pick between three and twenty winners in advance from a list of upcoming games; also known as "parlay cards."

BETTING LINE: The odds or the point spreads for an upcoming event. The betting line is what determines how a gambler wins or loses the bet and how much he wins or loses for every dollar wagered.

BLACK BOOK: A list of undesirable people who are forbidden to enter any casino in Nevada.

BLUE BOX: A device used by street bookmakers to make illegal long-distance calls.

(THE) BOARD: The location where betting odds are displayed in a Vegas sportsbook. In sports betting, "the board" also refers to the entire list of all the games. A gambler might say, "Give me the lines on the whole board, please."

BOOK: A group that accepts bets and wagers on the outcome of sporting events.

BOOKIE: Short for "bookmaker," the person who takes wagers and bets from sports bettors.

BOTTOM SHEET: A bookmaker's list of gambling debts for the week or month, depending on his settlement schedules.

BUCK: $100; also called a "dollar." When a gambler says, "Give me the Jets for a buck," he's betting $100.

CANADIAN LINE: The Canadian type of hockey betting line in which a combination of goals and a money line is used.

(THE) CHALK: The favorite in a race or a game.

CHALK PLAYER: A bettor who usually only wagers on the favorite teams and hardly ever on the underdogs. We have another word for that: suckers!

CIRCLED GAME: An event or game in which only limited action is accepted. Usually happens only when a star player is injured.

CLERK: The person who answers the phones and writes the bets or enters them into the computer on behalf of the bookmaker.

CLOSING LINE: The final list of point spreads offered in Las Vegas before the games start.

COVER: To win the game or event by the required number of points according to the betting line. This is also referred to as "covering the spread."

DAILY DOUBLE: A wager on the winners of two consecutive horse races. In Costa Rica "daily double" also means banging your wife and your secretary!

DEAD HEAT: In a horse race, when two or more horses finish in a tie.

DIME: $1,000; also referred to as ten "bucks" or ten "dollars."

DOG: The underdog team according to the betting line in an event or game.

DOG PLAYER: A bettor who mostly wagers on the underdog, rarely betting on a favorite.

DOLLAR: $100. A bettor who says, "Give me the Colts -6 for a dollar please," has just placed a $100 bet.

EARN: The percentage earned theoretically on every dollar spent on a particular type of bet. The hold on straight betting in sports is 5 percent. Also referred to as "the hold percentage."

EDGE: An unfair advantage that you believe might improve your ability to predict the outcome of a game or event. Card counting in blackjack gives an edge to the player.

EVEN MONEY: A wager with no point spread.

EXOTIC BET: Any bet other than a straight bet; usually a teaser, parlay, round robin, "if" bet, etc. In horse racing an exotic bet is any bet other than a win-place-or-show bet.

FALL GUY: The person who, whether guilty or innocent himself, accepts the full blame for a crime in order to protect others.

FALSE FAVORITE: A favorite in an event that some gamblers feel is outclassed by the competition.

FAVORITE: Team or person most likely to win the game or event according to the betting odds.

FIGURE: Amount of money owed by or to a bookmaker.

FIGURE MAN: Before the advent of computers, the person whose job was to score the betting tickets in a bookmaking operation.

FIN: $50.

FIXED GAME: A game in which one or more participants willfully manipulate the final outcome for money.

FLIP: To turn state's evidence. You never fucking flip. Period.

FRONT MAN: A person who has a facade of legitimacy but secretly represents the interests of his underworld backers.

FUTURES: Lines posted on games in the distant future— such as the Super Bowl, the NBA Championship, the Stanley Cup, or the World Series.

GETTING DOWN: Making a bet in time.

GREASE: A bribe.

HANDICAPPER: A person who rates and bets on sporting events for himself or for clients.

HANDLE: Total amount of bets taken.

HEDGE: To place bets on the opposite side to either minimize loss or guarantee winning.

HIGH ROLLER: A high-stakes gambler.

HOLDING YOUR OWN: Breaking even on a bet, neither winning nor losing. Has nothing to do with masturbation.

HOME-FIELD ADVANTAGE: The advantage or edge a team is expected to have as a result of playing on its home field.

HOT GAME: A game on which a betting syndicate is betting.

HOUSE: The operator of a gambling business.

"IF" BETS: A combination bet of anywhere from two to five straight bets joined by a condition. There are two types:

1. **SINGLE ACTION:** The bettor has action on the second straight bet *only if the first play wins.*

2. **DOUBLE ACTION:** The bettor has action on the second play *only if the first play wins, ties, or the game is canceled.*

INJURY REPORT: A description of the status of injured players; frequently used as a variable in betting equations.

INSIDE INFORMATION: The data obtained on a particular team, its players, or staff that may unfairly aid a gambler in betting on the final outcome of a game.

JUICE: The commission paid by a gambler on a lost sports bet. This is the bookie's fee.

LAY: To bet.

LAY A PRICE: Bet a favorite.

LAYING THE POINTS: Wagering on the favorite.

LAYING WOOD: Laying points in a bet or betting the favorite. Not a college expression for sex.

LAY OFF: Aside from being my wife's favorite term in bed, a bookmaker "lays off" when he bets with another book-maker to help equalize the excess action he has accepted from his customers.

LINE: The odds or point spread for a game.

LINEMAKER: The original person who establishes the betting lines in Vegas.

LOAN SHARK: Someone, usually mob-connected, who loans money at a high weekly interest rate.

LOCK: A sure thing; an easy winner.

L2Y: The last two years—how an operation did for the last twenty-four months.

LY: Last year—how an operation did for the last twelve months.

MARKER: A credit advance at a casino.

MIDDLE: To win both sides of the same betting proposition. This can be done if you bet certain odds with one sportsbook and then the opposite odds with another sportsbook at different lines.

MONEY LINE: The amount you must risk on a favorite to win $100, or the amount you win on an underdog if you risk $100.

MOVING THE LINE: A bookie making alterations to the line based on the volume of betting or other factors, such as injuries.

NEWSPAPER LINE: The betting line posted in the newspapers. In the age of "real time" and the Internet, be aware that these lines are often inaccurate and misleading.

NL: No line.

ODDS: The ratio of money that might be won or lost versus the amount of money bet.

ODDSMAKER: The person who establishes the betting lines; also referred to as the linesmaker.

OFF THE BOARD: A game on which the sportsbook will not accept action.

OPENING LINE: The initial Las Vegas point spreads for upcoming games.

OTB: Off-track betting.

OUT: A bookmaker or any source for getting a bet down.

OUTLAW LINE: The early, private line set by professional gamblers, which is financed, distributed, and enforced by the betting syndicates.

OVERLAY: When the odds are in favor of the bettor, not the sportsbook.

OVER/UNDER: The combined total of the points scored by the two teams.

PARLAY: A type of bet in which the bettor wagers on two to eight teams. As the number of teams increases (and your chances of winning decrease), your payouts get bigger. To win the parlay, all the bettor's chosen teams must win.

PARLAY CARDS: Cards distributed by bookies that allow gamblers to conveniently bet on parlays of up to fifteen positions.

PAST-POST: To unfairly make a bet after an event has started.

PIGEON: An uneducated, naive, or unsophisticated gambler. Also known as a sucker.

PLAYER: A gambler.

POINT SPREAD: The number of points by which a favorite must win to cover the bet; only used in betting on football and basketball.

POWER RATING: A number created by a handicapper on the basis of the strength of a particular team.

PRESS: To increase your wager.

PRICE: The lines or the point spread.

PRICEMAKER: An oddsmaker.

PUPPY: The underdog.

PUSH: A tie; neither side wins the game. All money is returned to the bettors.

ROUND ROBIN: A type of parlay bet in which all possible parlay combinations of the teams (from three to six) are selected.

RUNDOWN: For a particular sport, the list of all lines, totals, odds, point spreads, money lines, etc.

RUN LINE: An alternative line used in baseball betting based on runs rather than money lines.

RUNNER: Not Carl Lewis, but he'd be fucking great at this. Someone who makes your bets for you, a runner is like a bet messenger.

SHARP, OR SHARPIE: Smart bettor, possibly a professional.

SHAVING POINTS: Manipulating the outcome of a game so that the final score does not cover the spread.

SKIM: The cash siphoned off from an operation before it is noticed or accounted for.

SPECIAL TEASER: Type of teaser in which the more teams a player chooses, the more points are credited per team. The player can pick from two to four teams. All teams must cover the adjusted spreads to win the teaser.

SPORTSBOOK: A legal sports bookmaking business, like those in Las Vegas.

SPREAD: The point spread; lines.

SQUARE: Unsophisticated gambler; pigeon; sucker.

STEAM: Heavy action on one side of the game. Games that have steam don't necessarily reflect the sharper side.

STORE: A bookmaking operation.

STRAIGHT BET: A bet on a team to win.

STRAW MAN: A front man.

SUCKER BET: A bet type with a large edge to the sportsbook.

TAKING POINTS: Betting on the underdog.

TAPPED OUT: Broke.

TEASER: A bet type in which the bettor is required to bet on two to six teams while being given additional points. The bettor must win all games to win the bet.

THROWN GAME: A game lost intentionally by a participant.

TOTAL: The total combined point/runs/goals scored in a game.

TOUT SERVICE: A business that sells its expertise on sporting events.

UNDERDOG: The team most likely to lose the game according to the betting odds.

UNDERLAY: When the odds on a bet favor the sportsbook.

UNNATURAL MONEY: Large wagers that suddenly appear against the conventional wisdom of the oddsmakers and handicappers.

VALUE: The team or bet with the highest possible edge.

VIG, OR VIGORISH: The "juice" on a bet—the bookie's fee.

WAGER LIMIT: Maximum bet accepted by the sportsbook before the price will be changed.

WAGERING STAMP: A federal occupational tax for gamblers.

WELCH: To refuse to pay off a bet already made and lost.

CASINO TERMS

Las Vegas, where I served two years at Caesar's Palace for Caesar himself, was the cornerstone of my corporate training. I excelled at it because of my gambling background and electric vibe and personality, but also because I was aware of what I wanted and I was willing to go get it. Las Vegas was made for people like me, and I took full advantage of that when the right opportunity presented itself. Operating in Las Vegas is unlike anything you have ever experienced anywhere else in the world. Following is a glossary of terms and phrases both technical and loose. Study it hard so you can sound like a pro.

ACTIVE PLAYER: A player with money at risk.

ALL-IN: In card-room poker, to call with (to bet) all your chips; also known as "going all-in."

ANTE: In card games, a bet required to begin a hand. The initial compulsory bet before you receive your cards in casino stud poker.

ARM: A player who is so skilled at throwing the dice that he seems to be able to alter the conventional odds of the game. Whether or not such individuals actually exist or are simply the product of game legend is debatable. However, it is worth noting that casino craps dealers are very adamant about both dice being thrown against the far wall of the table to ensure a completely random outcome. I guess they aren't going to take any chances.

BACCARAT: Also called punto banco and chemin de fer, baccarat is a nonskill game that oddly enough is enjoyed most by the intellectual elite. Go figure!

BANKER: The dealer. In some card games a player can become a banker/dealer in turn.

BANKROLL: The total amount of money that either the player or the casino has on hand to back his wagering activities; also known as "roll" or "wad."

BARRED: Permanently banned from entering the casino premises.

BEEF: A dispute or claim involving a player and his bookmaker or a casino dealer. A dispute over the outcome of a bet. A problematic situation involving a bet.

BLACK BOOK: The list of undesirable people who are forbidden to enter any casino in Nevada.

BLIND BET: A bet made by a player without seeing his card.

BUG: A joker.

BUMP: To raise. (Unless you are in the bathroom with a blonde at the Skybar—then a bump is something else.)

BURN CARDS: The cards that are removed from the top of the deck, not to be dealt, and placed in the discard tray after a shuffle and cut.

BUY IN: The amount of cash used by a player to purchase casino chips before he starts playing a table game.

CAGE: The casino cashier who cashes in your chips, posts up your funds, or settles your credit.

CAMOUFLAGE: Various tricks used by a professional cheat to conceal his activities from the casino and avoid scrutiny, including pretending to bet like a typical gambler to conceal his edge, using disguises, and appearing to be drunk.

CAPPING: When a cheat places extra chips on top of the initial bet after the deal has begun.

CARD COUNTING: In blackjack games, memorizing the played cards to establish when a conditional probability advantage exists on the remaining cards against the dealer so as to bet higher during those periods of advantage. Casinos have put in seven-deck shufflers to combat this form of advanced strategy.

CARD SHARK: An expert at cards.

CAROUSEL: A group of slot machines positioned in a ring, with a change girl standing in the center.

CARPET JOINT: A luxury Vegas casino like the Bellagio.

CASE MONEY: Emergency "under the bed" money.

CASINO RATE: A reduced hotel-room rate that the casinos offer to good customers who don't qualify for full comps.

CHASE: Trying to get back lost money on a bet by following it ("chasing" it) with a rushed bet.

CHECKS: Another term for a chip.

CHIPS: Round plastic discs with denominational value. Casinos require that chips, not cash, be used for betting. They are purchased at the gaming tables and exchanged at the cage.

CHIP TRAY: The tray in front of a dealer that holds that table's chip supply.

(RIDING HIS) COATTAIL: Betting the same numbers as another bettor who is hot.

COLD: A player on a losing streak. A table or slot machine that is not paying out.

COLOR UP: This has nothing to do with getting hookers downtown. To color up is to exchange smaller-denomination chips for larger-denomination chips, usually upon leaving the table after a big win. Though coloring up makes it easier to carry the chips, what it really is for—and most players don't know this—is to allow the casino a final chance to count and record the player's chip activity.

COMPS: Complimentary gifts given by the casino to entice players to gamble. Typical comps include RFB (free Room, Food, and Beverages).

CRACKING THE NUT: This has nothing to do with the porn pay-per-view in the hotel room. To crack the nut is to make enough money on a gambling venture to cover all expenses plus a reasonable net profit.

CRAPS: Casino dice table-game traditionally played by screaming men who take full advantage of every opportunity to high-five, twist, and shout out things like, "You eleven," and, "Winner-winner chicken dinner!"

CREDITS: With slot machines, wagers are expressed in credits. One credit equals one unit.

CROSSROADER: An old '60s casino term used to describe a cheat. It originated long before the 1960s in the Old West, where gambling saloons were located at crossroads. The term is still used today by the old-timers who work in Vegas to describe casino cheats.

CROUPIER: French word for "dealer."

DEUCE: A two in dice.

DICE: Two identical-numbered cubes; used in craps.

DIE: The inevitable outcome for your casino bankroll, yes, but also the singular form of "dice."

DOUBLE OR NOTHING: Famous last words! An even-money bet that is twice the amount of the last losing bet made.

DOUBLING DOWN: A betting option in blackjack where the player doubles his bet and is dealt one card only.

DOUBLING UP: Doubling the size of the previous bet in the hope of winning back the money lost or increasing the profit made.

DOWN CARD: The dealer's facedown card in blackjack.

DOWN TO THE FELT: Broke; out of bankroll.

DROP: Money lost.

DROP BOX: On a gaming table, the box that serves as a repository for cash, markers, and casino chips.

EVEN MONEY BET: A bet with one-to-one odds—that is, a bet that pays you back the same amount you wagered plus your original wager.

EXPECTED WIN RATE: In slot machines, the theoretical percentage of the total amount of money wagered that you can expect to win back over time.

EYE IN THE SKY: Slang for the video surveillance cameras used by casinos to monitor the gaming area for cheats.

FACE CARDS: The jack, queen, and king of any suit of cards.

FIRING: Betting a lot. A player who is firing is wagering large sums.

FIRST BASE: At the blackjack table, the position on the far left of the dealer; first base is the first position to be dealt cards.

FISH: A sucker; a big loser. I always say that if you can't spot the fish at the table, just look in the mirror.

FLAT BETTING: Betting the same amount on each wager, never raising or lowering the bet.

FLAT TOP: When a slot machine's jackpot is a fixed amount rather than a progressive amount.

FLEA: An annoying person who wants something for nothing. For instance, someone who expects to be comped by the hotel when he is not a big enough gambler.

FRONT MONEY: Cash or bank checks/wires deposited with the casino cage by a player to establish a line against which he can sign markers at the tables to receive chips and bet.

GAMBLERS' ANONYMOUS: A support group that assists problem gamblers and addicted/compulsive gamblers. If you are reading this far into the glossary, it might be worth looking into!

GREASE: A bribe.

GROSS WINNINGS: The total payout (including your stake or risk).

HAND: The cards you hold. Also refers to everything that happens within a shuffle of blackjack or a roll of the dice. You might say, "I did okay for that hand."

HARD COUNT: A casino counting up the money—mostly the change from slot machines—that it made in a day, usually in a special room under tight security.

HARD-WAY BET: A craps bet in which the two dice must land on doubles to win. There are only four hard-way combinations: hard four (two-and-two), hard six (three-and-three), hard eight (four-and-four), and hard ten (five-and-five). It is called the hard way because it is harder to make, for instance, a four-and-four as an eight than it is to make any combination of six-and-two or five-and-three.

HIGH ROLLER: A player who makes big bets; a whale.

HIT: In blackjack, to take another card. Not to be confused with the ordering of a death or the smoking of a joint.

HOLDING YOUR OWN: Neither winning nor losing but breaking even. This is the term most husbands use on the second day of the trip when telling their wives how they are doing, well after they have already lost both the mortgage and car payment.

HOLE CARD: In blackjack, the facedown card that the dealer gets. In stud and hold 'em poker, the facedown cards dealt to each player.

HOT: A player on a winning streak. A slot machine that is paying out. A loud craps table.

HOUSE: The operators of a gambling game.

HOUSE EDGE: The casino percentage advantage, gained by paying less than the true odds.

INSURANCE: In blackjack, a side bet that the dealer has a natural twenty-one. Insurance is offered only when the dealer's up card is an ace. The insurance bet wins double if the dealer has a natural, but loses if the dealer does not. Like flood insurance in the desert, it's never a good bet.

JACKPOT: A big purse or win on a slot machine.

LADDERMAN: A casino employee who oversees the baccarat game, usually from a chair above the table.

(TABLE) LAYOUT: The cloth on a gaming table and the markings that tell you where you can place your bets.

LOAD UP: To play the maximum number of coins per spin allowed by a slot machine or video game.

LOBBY: A place to find hookers.

LOOSE: Except when discussing the flight attendants on first-class flights to Vegas, a reference to slot machines that have a generous payout.

MARKER: A check/IOU that can be written at the gaming table by a player who has established credit with the casino or posted up money in the cage.

MECHANIC: A dealer who cheats by using sleight of hand to prearrange the cards.

MINI-BACCARAT: A scaled-down, low-stakes version of baccarat in which the players can't touch the cards.

MONEY PUT IN ACTION: Money that was at risk on the table during the hand.

NATURAL: This has nothing to do with blond pussy hair. In blackjack, a natural is a two-card hand of twenty-one points. In baccarat, a natural is a two-card total of eight or nine.

NUT: Either the overhead costs of running a casino or the fixed amount a gambler decides to risk in a day.

ODDS: Ratio of probabilities. The casino's view, based on the math, of the chance of a player winning.

ON TILT: When a gambler has a bad reaction to an unlucky hand and the result is an uncontrolled wild play.

PAINT: A jack, queen, or king. Also known as a picture card or a face card.

PALETTE: The tool (usually a long flat wooden baton) used in the baccarat game to house and move cards on the table.

PASS: In card games, to not bet; to fold. In dice, to reject the opportunity to shoot the dice.

PAYOUT: The amount of money paid out to a player as a win.

PIT: The area of a casino in which a group of table games are arranged and the center area is restricted to dealers and other authorized casino personnel.

PIT BOSS: The pit supervisor. Usually oversees many tables at the same time.

PIT MANAGER: The casino employee in charge of enforcing casino policy at all the table games. He deals with any problems that may arise, including crucial decisions that may make a customer dissatisfied or angry. He also handles comps by ducking and dodging fleas who are trying to get a free room.

POINT (THE): The number established on the come-out roll of a crap game.

POT: Besides a reference to my preferred medicine, the amount of money in a poker game that accumulates in the middle of the table as each player antes, bets, and raises. The pot goes to the winner of the hand.

PRESS: Adding the winnings over the current bet to increase your next wager.

PROGRESSIVE: A connected group of slot machines whose potential jackpot increases with each coin that is played. When the progressive jackpot finally hits, the amount resets to the starting number.

RACINOS: Racetrack casinos.

RACK: A plastic container in which you can transport large-denomination coins, slot machine tokens, and casino chips.

RAKE: The money the casino charges for each hand of poker, usually a percentage (5 to 10 percent) or a flat fee taken from the pot after each round of betting.

RATED: Determination by the casino of the comps a player deserves based on his play or action.

RFB: The free Room, Food, and Beverages offered by a hotel to a player in exchange for his promise to gamble.

SAWBUCK: $10.

SAWDUST JOINT: Old-timers' term for a nonluxury casino.

SCARED MONEY: Money that a player cannot afford to lose and that makes him nervous. They say that "scared money don't make none."

SESSION: A period of play for a gambler.

SHARK: A good and crafty player who may pose as a novice early in the game.

SHARP: An astute and educated bettor.

SHILL: A person who plays in the game for the house, club, or casino to fill empty seats until more real players join in.

SHINER: A tiny mirror or any reflecting device used by a cheater to get a look at the dealer's hole card.

SHOE: A device, usually a wooden box, used for holding and dispensing playing cards to be dealt. Shoe games typically use six or eight decks of cards. Blackjack and baccarat are the most popular shoe games.

SHORT RUN: A short series of winning wagers.

(CARD) SHUFFLING: The card-mixing techniques used to prepare a deck or a shoe for continued play.

SILVER MINING: Looking for coins left in unattended slot machines; also called "slot walking."

SKIN: $1.

SKIN GAME: A game with two or more cheaters working together and waiting for "johns."

SKOON: $1.

SNAKE EYES: Rolling a two in craps. It's called snake eyes because the dice look like eyes and because, like a snake, the roll is usually bad news for the player.

SOFT HAND: The effect of three days and all the moisturizer you can use at the Bellagio? Not quite. In blackjack, any hand that contains an ace counted as eleven.

SPINNER: A winning streak.

STACK: A stack of chips, usually twenty chips in a column.

STANDING HAND: In blackjack, a hand with which the player is expected to stand.

STEAMING: When a player, frustrated with how badly a session of play is going, has lost emotional control and is betting more aggressively and often recklessly in an attempt to turn things around.

STREAK BETTING: Raising or lowering the size of your wager based on what happened on the previous round or rounds; also know as "progressive betting."

SURRENDER: What you have done each time you walk into that casino. Also an option in blackjack to give up half your bet for the privilege of not playing out a hand.

SYSTEM: A method of betting, usually mathematically based, used by a bettor to try to get an advantage. A prominent factor in most systems is the criterion the player uses to determine when he should raise or lower his wagers.

TABLE HOLD: The amount of money won by the casino table game from the players during a complete work shift.

TAPPING OUT: Losing your entire gambling bankroll and thus having to stop playing.

TRUE ODDS: The real odds of something happening; actual odds. The odds posted in a casino are never the true odds.

VIP: A Very Important Person. Usually a big bettor or a high roller.

WHALE: A player who makes extremely large wagers. Unlike high rollers, who consistently wager $100 or more per round, whales are typically those who make wagers amounting to thousands per round, if not tens or hundreds of thousands of dollars.

WHITE MEAT: Profit.

DRUG TERMS

So why the word "drugs" in the title? Pot is a drug. I smoked more pot than the 320 employees I had combined, and I was sharper than all of them at all times. I was like a cross between Bob Marley and Steve Wynn. I started smoking weed when I was eighteen years old. The good thing is that I was mature enough at eighteen to realize that weed is serious enough that it needs to be respected. When you are fourteen and you smoke weed, you always wind up doing blow by sixteen and then smoking rock by eighteen, and if you're lucky you die young, because living life addicted to crack is way worse. There is my message to young adults. Don't be stupid and let pot talk you into more serious drugs; it is a game you will lose every time.

I was smart to never let it get much further than weed when it came to drugs, but not smart enough. While rocking out with my band in the early '90s, I experimented with Ecstasy, acid, and mushrooms. I loved Ecstasy. I mean, I loved everyone when I was on Ecstasy. After thirty days straight of doing five hits a day, I was sick of loving. I wanted to hate again. I wanted my old cynical self back. I walked into the room of twelve friends who were crashing and grinding their teeth in my living room. They were lying there sweating like beasts. I had told them all individually and as a group how I loved them and cared for them all like brothers while I was tripping hard on the love drug the night before. I stood up on the couch and announced at the top of my lungs that the party was over, that I didn't love anyone anymore, and that we weren't blood brothers. I told everyone they had fifteen minutes to wake up and get the fuck out before I got my gun and started shooting up the fucking room. After thirty days of extreme bliss and love-making with both hot chicks and very ugly and fat chicks (when you're on Ecstasy you love and fuck them all), I was ready to start my journey back to normalcy. My plan was to smoke a ton of pot to ease the transition from utopia back to planet earth. I smoked ten joints a day for eighteen months straight, and it really worked. In fact, it worked so well that it is fifteen years later and the plan hasn't changed a bit.

Here is a list of words we use when we talk about our weed.

BAGGY: Small bag of weed.

BAKED: Really high.

BIG BOY: A pound of weed.

BLAZE: Smokin' weed.

BLITZED: Really high.

BLIZZY: Blunt.

BLUNT: Taking a cigar, cutting it open, emptying out all the tobacco, filling it with weed, resealing, and lighting it up!

BONG: Water pipe.

CHEEBA: Weed.

CHILLY BILLY: A bong filled with ice chips instead of water.

CLAM BAKE: Smoking weed in a closed area like a car.

CREEPER: Weed that takes a while before you feel anything.

DIRT WEED: Bad-quality weed.

GANJA: Weed.

GHOST HIT: Holding in a hit so long that when you exhale nothing comes out.

HASH: A weed by-product collected from the resins and flowers of the female plant to form an intense, high-powered Tootsie Roll of joy.

HASH OIL: Very potent oil derived from the hash-making process. Usually contains up to 97 percent THC (delta-9-tetrahydracannabinol).

HERB: Weed.

HOOKAH: Middle Eastern water pipe.

JAY: Joint.

JOINT: A cannabis cigarette.

KIEF: The powder crumbs in the bottom of a baggy.

LIGHTWEIGHT: Someone who gets high really fast.

MUNCHIES: When you smoke weed and get really hungry.

OZ: An ounce of weed.

QP: A quarter-pound of weed.

SACK: A bag of weed.

SHOTGUN: The hole in a bong or pipe used to get better hits.

SPLIFF: Jamaican term for joint.

THC: Delta-9-tetrahydracannabinol.

THE MILE HIGH: The high you get when you smoke weed in Denver.

WAKE AND BAKE: When you smoke weed first thing in the morning right after you get up.

Acknowledgments

FIRST, I ACKNOWLEDGE Jesus Christ as my personal Lord and savior. I thank God for my entire journey. Whatever road I had to travel to get to where I am today was well worth the often bumpy ride.

I want to thank these people: My wife Melisse for being my partner in crime. Without her, I am nothing. My children Jackie, Juliette, and Jace—it is all for them. The incredibly talented author Bob Schaller, and now my dear friend, for the entire creative experience. I am so lucky to have worked with you on this project. My current Stevo Inc. staff of Sam Weston, Mark Greenhaus, Toni Pelmeri, and Taylor Abramson for assisting me, supporting me, and, most importantly, putting up with me throughout this entire book process. My main man BoneCrusher: rest in peace, brother. Your picture is on my wall. Al Rollie, you are the man; thank you for being my partner and friend, and thank you for your assistance with the book. To every employee, affiliate, or partner I've ever had, I hope I mean as much to you as you all do to me. We are more than just work acquaintances, we are family too, and I love you all very much.

Thanks also to my friends and family: Kenny O'Connor, Dave Budin, Rita Budin, Robin Budin, Stacie Budin, Jessie and Kimberley Budin, Phil Budin, Rex (RIP), Hubie (RIP), Lyle Chariff, Sandy Becher, Ronnie Sussman, Stu Feiner, Brandon Lang, Steve Rattner, Eduardo Herrera, Dave Kaplan, Jason Port, Sherm, Ian Horowitz, Sol Lallouz, Pascal Lasry, Raymond Slate, Naoum Zarcadoolas, Darren Davis, Danny Norten, Vinnie Perez, Uly Busch, Bob and Julie Fiume, Carley and Megan, Claudia Jagid, Nanci Iadorola, Leo, Cookie, Vegas Phil, Joey Crutel, Rocky Stein, Richard Nemec, Peter Gold, Goldie, Harvey Greenburg, Ralph Hunter, Steve Arintok, Dino, Daryll, Magda, Jerry Tannenbaum, Pat and John, Kobi Karp, Lisi Port, Luby, William Ramirez, Rich Groden, Lana Bernstein, Melissa Katz, Macalousos, Ronnie Bulldog, Steve Ganz, Tim O'Neal, Alan Richardson, Renee, William Sanchez, Dan Zucker, Brad Beckerman, Joey Krutel, and Jimmy Shapiro.

Our literary agent, Bob Diforio, found the right home at Skyhorse Publishing with Mark Weinstein, my editor, and for that I thank both gentlemen.